SOCIAL SECURITY

FROM **MEDICARE** TO **SPOUSAL**
BENEFITS, AN ESSENTIAL PRIMER ON
GOVERNMENT RETIREMENT AID

101

ALFRED MILL with MICHELE CAGAN, CPA

ADAMS MEDIA

NEW YORK   LONDON   TORONTO   SYDNEY   NEW DELHI

Adams Media
An Imprint of Simon & Schuster, LLC
100 Technology Center Drive
Stoughton, Massachusetts 02072

This Adams Media hardcover edition
October 2024
First Adams Media hardcover edition
October 2016

ADAMS MEDIA and colophon are registered
trademarks of Simon & Schuster, LLC.

Simon & Schuster: Celebrating 100 Years of
Publishing in 2024

For information about special discounts
for bulk purchases, please contact Simon &
Schuster Special Sales at 1-866-506-1949 or
business@simonandschuster.com.

The Simon & Schuster Speakers Bureau can
bring authors to your live event. For more
information or to book an event, contact
the Simon & Schuster Speakers Bureau at
1-866-248-3049 or visit our website at
www.simonspeakers.com.

Manufactured in the United States of
America

1 2024

Library of Congress Cataloging-in-
Publication Data
Names: Mill, Alfred, author. | Cagan,
Michele, author.
Title: Social security 101, 2nd edition /
Alfred Mill with Michele Cagan, CPA.
Description: 2nd edition. | Stoughton,
Massachusetts: Adams Media, [2024] |
Includes index.

Identifiers: LCCN 2024019295 | ISBN
9781507222348 (hc) | ISBN 9781507222355
(ebook)
Subjects: LCSH: Social security--United
States--Handbooks, manuals, etc. | Old
age pensions--United States--Handbooks,
manuals, etc. | Retirement income--United
States--Handbooks, manuals, etc. |
Medicare--Handbooks, manuals, etc.
Classification: LCC HD7125 .M49 2024 |
DDC 368.4/300973--dc23/eng/2024
LC record available at https://lccn.loc
.gov/2024019295

ISBN 978-1-5072-2234-8
ISBN 978-1-5072-2235-5 (ebook)

Contains material adapted from the
following titles published by Adams Media,
an Imprint of Simon & Schuster, LLC: *Social
Security 101* by Alfred Mill, copyright
© 2016, ISBN 978-1-4405-9922-4; *The
Everything® Retirement Planning Book* by
Judith B. Harrington and Stanley
J. Steinberg, CFP, copyright © 2007, ISBN
978-1-59869-207-5; and *The Everything®
Personal Finance in Your 20s & 30s Book, 3rd
Edition* by Howard Davidoff, JD, CPA, LLM,
copyright © 2012, ISBN 978-1-4405-4256-5.

CONTENTS

INTRODUCTION 5

INTRODUCTION

When you think about funding your retirement (whether you plan to retire soon or many years from now), Social Security is likely one of the main financial benefits that comes to mind. The majority of Americans pay into Social Security—a program that provides steady pay for disabled or retired people—throughout their working lives. Around 40% of US retirees depend on Social Security payments as their sole income during retirement. While Social Security can be tough to navigate, understanding the ins and outs of this program will help you prepare for retirement and receive more money overall.

With *Social Security 101, 2nd Edition*, you'll have access to the most up-to-date information about this government program, including details on how to apply for benefits and when you should start taking them. Additionally, you'll learn important strategies to maximize the benefits you receive, updates to Social Security laws, and changes that affect your filing plans, as well as guidance on the prevalence of new Social Security scams (and how to protect yourself from them), and how Americans' increased life expectancy has impacted Social Security. Plus, you'll find information about:

- How to handle government taxes in relation to Social Security
- What benefits are available to your spouse or children
- When to take benefits, and the consequences you'll face if you take them too early

- How to appeal the system if it works against you
- How to plan for tomorrow, and the possibility for changes to Social Security benefits
- And more!

While Social Security is important for retirement, it's also important for those who have differing personal or monetary factors. *Social Security 101, 2nd Edition* explains how to approach the many facets of the program depending on your background—for example, if you are disabled, self-employed, or looking for spousal benefits, Social Security will work differently for you and your family. Additionally, you'll learn more about the government healthcare programs, Medicare and Medicaid, and how they relate to your Social Security benefits.

Social Security is an important component of a carefully thought-out retirement plan. Each section in this book is designed to teach you about how Social Security works, ensuring you receive all the money that's due to come your way. Plus, you'll get real-world examples of how Social Security impacts all aspects of daily life—from saving on costly medical prescriptions, to calculating your pension in relation to Social Security, to information on the SECURE Act. With each new detail in these pages, you'll expand your Social Security tool kit, allowing you to confidently build your financially secure retirement. So, let's begin!

WHAT IS SOCIAL SECURITY?

A Retirement Plan for Everyone

Although you may not think about Social Security when you join the workforce, the Social Security Administration (SSA) has always accounted for you.

When you receive your first paycheck, you step into the complex government program called Social Security. For the rest of your working career, that program tracks you. And when you finally decide to retire at the age of sixty-two or older, you'll apply to the SSA for the benefits you've accumulated in the course of your working life.

As you begin to approach your full retirement age (more about that later), you'll probably give more and more thought to Social Security, asking questions like:

- How much are my benefits per month going to amount to?
- What if it's not enough for me to live on?
- I keep hearing that Social Security is going bankrupt. What if all the money's gone by the time I retire?
- Where can I go for help in figuring this stuff out?

These are all good questions, and there are certainly plenty of others. Social Security has been around for a long time, and it's seen its fair share of changes and adjustments. This has led to a seemingly byzantine set of rules and regulations. You'll learn more about this soon, but for now, the important thing is for you to understand what Social Security is.

SOCIAL INSURANCE

At its most basic definition, Social Security is a form of social insurance that is set up and administered by the US government. Payments to you from the system can begin as early as age sixty-two (although there are good reasons not to take your benefits that early) and will continue until you die. It's essentially a government-run retirement program that aims to keep retirees out of poverty.

The program is funded through taxes, which are collected directly from workers' paychecks. Look on your latest paycheck stub and find the acronym FICA. The amount next to it is how much money from your paycheck went toward Social Security.

FICA and SECA

FICA stands for Federal Insurance Contributions Act. The Social Security tax is also sometimes designated SECA, which stands for Self-Employment Contributions Act. This latter tax is levied on people who are self-employed (as the name implies). Some portion of both taxes also goes toward the governmental medical program, Medicare.

Payouts from the Social Security program are huge. According to the Social Security Administration, about 67 million people in the United States received Social Security benefits in 2023. Total payouts through the program amounted to almost $1.4 trillion for that year. The number of people receiving Social Security benefits is expected to rise as members of the baby boom generation continue to retire, something that has created concerns that the program might go bankrupt.

This will be examined in more detail later, including the possible ways in which Social Security might be fixed. For now, let's look at the program as it currently exists.

The taxes collected through workers' paychecks go into one of a series of trust funds: The Federal Old-Age and Survivors Insurance Trust Fund, the Federal Disability Insurance Trust Fund, the Federal Hospital Insurance Trust Fund, and the Federal Supplemental Medical Insurance Trust Fund. Your earnings are taxed for these funds up to a certain federally determined limit. As of 2024, the maximum amount of taxable income was $168,600. Any money you make beyond that cap isn't taxed for Social Security (although, of course, it is taxed in other ways such as income tax and Medicare).

The SSA also operates other important programs, including the Children's Health Insurance Program (CHIP) and Supplemental Security Income (SSI). The SSA, which has its headquarters in Maryland, has ten regional offices scattered around the United States and employs more than 60,000 people.

Some Facts and Figures

Here are some things you may not know about Social Security:

- Nine out of ten people aged sixty-five and older receive Social Security benefits.
- Social Security covers an estimated 181 million workers (in the sense that anyone who pays payroll taxes to Social Security is "covered").
- Of those receiving benefits, 51.3 million get retirement benefits; 5.9 million receive survivors benefits; and 8.8 million receive disability benefits.
- About one in four of today's twenty-year-olds will become disabled before reaching age sixty-seven.
- In today's workforce, only about 21% of workers have private pension coverage.

The agency issues a nine-digit number to all US citizens and temporary working residents. This number is used to track people within the Social Security system, but it has also become an important identification number that is used in many circumstances to guarantee personal security (for instance, in banking transactions).

The way in which Social Security has been administered has changed over the years, reflecting changing economic circumstances within the country. The most recent policy change came in 2015, when Congress passed a law that eliminated several filing strategies (particularly the strategy called "file and suspend") that had been gaining in popularity.

Baby Names Lists

As a by-product of issuing Social Security numbers to newborns, the SSA keeps a list of popular baby names for any given year since the system started. Every year, the SSA issues two lists: one for the ten most popular girls' names and another for the ten most popular boys' names. Go to www.ssa.gov/OACT/babynames to check out the lists.

In general, Social Security mostly benefits lower-paid workers, since these are the people who are unlikely to be able to save enough for retirement on their own. However, anyone who pays into the system by working as an employee or who is self-employed and pays Social Security taxes can become eligible to receive benefits. This is a controversial aspect of the program, and some have suggested there should be an upper income level beyond which people wouldn't receive benefits (as they could likely afford to support themselves in retirement without government aid). Warren Buffett, one of the richest people in the world, has pointed out the absurdity that he receives Social Security benefits.

You're also eligible for benefits if you've just been released from prison. You can't receive benefits while you're in jail (provided you've been incarcerated for thirty continuous days), but once you're released, you can begin or restart your benefits.

In addition to paying out retirement checks, the Social Security Trust Funds also make payments to people who are disabled to the degree that they are unable to work. In 2022, this part of the funds made payments of around $143 billion. Another part of the program, the Supplemental Security Income (SSI), pays money to low-income people who are sixty-five or older, blind, or disabled. Some would argue that this isn't really part of the Social Security system, as it's funded from the general funds of US Treasury rather than the Social Security Trust Funds. However, these funds are still administered by the SSA.

THE BEGINNINGS OF SOCIAL SECURITY

Roots in the Great Depression

In the late 1920s Americans were convinced that they had life by the tail. It was the Jazz Age, the Roaring Twenties; bootlegged champagne flowed freely, and dancers puffed on cigarettes while downing that new American innovation, cocktails. Inventions such as the telephone, moving pictures, and above all, the automobile spread across the country, changing both the physical and cultural face of the United States. It was a prosperous time. World War I, which had devastated Europe, had barely touched the US. Far from the death and destruction of Europe, American factories turned out hundreds of millions of dollars in commodities that poured into eager markets.

The stock market was intoxicated by this wealth. Stock prices soared to higher and higher levels. Analysts predicted an endless bull market, and that prices would continue to rise.

However, beginning on October 24, 1929, the American stock market precipitously crashed. Over a two-day period, the Dow Jones Industrial Average fell 23%. The demand for manufactured goods dried up, seemingly overnight. Businesses collapsed, industries shrank, and millions were thrown out of work. President Herbert Hoover's responses to the economic chaos were simply not good enough. Across the country, homeless workers erected shantytowns named Hoovervilles. Whatever small nest eggs had been accumulated by workers for their old age were wiped out quickly. The public's anger with Hoover and the Republican Party helped sweep Franklin D. Roosevelt into the presidency in 1933.

A less likely champion of the common person could scarcely be imagined. Roosevelt came from an aristocratic clan that numbered President Theodore Roosevelt as its most distinguished member. Franklin's mother, Sara, came from a New York family whose fortune was founded on the opium trade with China. The young Franklin attended Groton School, a private school in Groton, Massachusetts, and then went on to Harvard. At some stage, he learned to sympathize with those who were less fortunate than him. This compassion for the poor and needy colored much of his political career.

Upon assuming the presidency, Roosevelt developed and expanded many programs begun by Hoover, and he also launched a series of new initiatives. Collectively, he dubbed this effort the New Deal. The New Deal was composed of two parts: The first part, the First New Deal from 1933–1934, is sometimes referred to as "The First Hundred Days," since the laws that created the new programs were passed during the first one hundred days of Roosevelt's administration. In this First New Deal period, the president's actions focused on unemployment and the need for immediate relief for poverty-stricken workers. During the Second New Deal, which lasted from 1935–1936, Roosevelt was able to contemplate the economy and the country in a broader, more leisured perspective.

With the issues of poverty and joblessness on his mind, Roosevelt was disturbed to see that Dr. Francis Townsend had proposed a plan for the government to take care of people in their old age. Townsend proposed the government pay everyone over sixty years old a monthly sum of $200. His only restriction was that they should not have a criminal past.

Townsend's proposal was extremely popular, and Roosevelt was concerned he needed a viable alternative before the 1936 presidential election. So, he asked Secretary of Labor Frances Perkins to come up with a plan to counter Townsend's.

Perkins and the committee that assisted her studied the issue from many different angles and eventually produced a report. The report, in turn, spurred the writing and passage of a bill in 1935: the Social Security Act.

Bismarck and the German Precedent

One of the important precedents studied by Perkins's committee was the social insurance created under German Chancellor Otto von Bismarck in the previous century. Though a die-hard conservative, Bismarck in 1889 set up a system of old-age insurance that required payments from both workers and employers. His goal was to prevent the implementation of some more radical scheme. When accused of socialism on account of his program, Bismarck could point to his long political record of hostility to socialism and communism.

THE SCOPE OF THE ACT

The 1935 law passed by Congress was limited in scope compared to what Social Security covers today. The preamble says the Act is:

An act to provide for the general welfare by establishing a system of Federal old-age benefits, and by enabling the several States to make more adequate provision for aged persons, blind persons, dependent and crippled children, maternal and child welfare, public health, and the administration of their unemployment compensation laws; to establish a Social Security Board; to raise revenue; and for other purposes.

The Act excluded almost half of US workers from Social Security coverage; only gradually did it expand to cover most of the population.

"We can never insure one hundred percent of the population against one hundred percent of the hazards and vicissitudes of life, but we have tried to frame a law which will give some measure of protection to the average citizen and to his family against the loss of a job and against poverty-ridden old age."

—President Franklin D. Roosevelt

The Social Security Administration, which grew out of the Social Security Board, was at first an independent agency. In 1939, it became part of the Federal Security Agency, a subcabinet department, but it resumed its status as an independent agency of the federal government in 1995.

John G. Winant

John G. Winant was the first head of the Social Security Board, charged with carrying out the provisions of the 1935 act. Winant was a former three-term governor of New Hampshire and a member of the Republican Party. When Alf Landon, the Republican Party's presidential candidate in the 1936 elections, began campaigning against Social Security, Winant resigned from the board in order to defend Social Security against Landon's attacks.

THE FIRST BENEFICIARIES

When the program formally began in 1937, employers and workers paid 1% tax each on the worker's income up to $3,000. Benefits began to be paid out in 1940 (they were originally scheduled for 1942 but were moved up by a 1939 amendment to the Act). In that year, Ernest Ackerman of Cleveland became the first person to receive a Social Security benefit—all of seventeen cents. His pay had been taxed five cents.

The first monthly payment went to Ida May Fuller of Vermont. Between 1937 and 1939 she paid in $24.75 to the system. Starting in January 1940 she received monthly benefits of $22.54. Since she lived to be one hundred years old, her benefits at the end of her life totaled $22,888.92.

Expanding Beneficiaries

In 1950, Congress expanded the range of people covered to include some agricultural workers, domestic workers, nonprofit employees, and those self-employed. By 1954, that range had grown to include all agricultural labor, hotel and laundry workers, and employees of state and local government. In the 1960s, the number of people covered continued to increase, including disabled adult children of workers covered under the Act. Today, as previously mentioned, an estimated 181 million workers are covered by Social Security—an impressive feat for a program more than eighty years old.

THE HISTORY OF RETIREMENT

The Evolution of Leisure

Social Security grew out of the Great Depression and the New Deal policies of Franklin D. Roosevelt's administration. It's now important to put this in a broader context to consider how the concept of life after work developed. This concept of retirement is a recent phenomenon that itself is closely linked to the move from an agrarian to an industrial society, paired with the tremendous strides in healthcare over the past century and a half.

Many people credit Otto von Bismarck, as chancellor of Germany in the late nineteenth century, with laying the groundwork for Social Security. In fact, Bismarck should be credited with developing the concept of retirement itself by establishing a pension for military personnel. He set the age at which a soldier could begin collecting his pension at sixty-five. That would be like setting the retirement age for today at 125 because, in that era, the average life expectancy for Germans was the mid-thirties. The actuarial number crunchers of that era would have had no problem with a pension as a concept under this age restriction because virtually no one would live that long.

When Social Security legislation was first passed in 1935, the age for receiving benefits was set at sixty-five. This sounds normal by today's standards, but what you might not know is that American life expectancy at that time was only sixty-two, meaning that the government had limited financial exposure with this sweeping program. Further, as the legislation was originally written, only about 60% of the working population—those in commerce and industry—qualified for Social Security. Plus, the first checks weren't distributed until 1940.

Expanding the Aging Population

Thanks to tremendous decreases in infant and child mortality through the first half of the twentieth century, the number of people alive today that are at least sixty-five years old is equal to half of all the people who have ever lived to age sixty-five in the course of written history.

In the 1950s, benefits were added to Social Security and the overall umbrella expanded to cover government employees, farmers, domestic help, and the self-employed. Additionally, new legislation stated that workers could begin receiving reduced benefits at age sixty-two if they chose. Women became eligible for benefits in 1961. In 1965, hospital benefits were added, which became the basis for the Medicare and Medicaid coverage that today's seniors are fighting to protect. Social Security changes continued through the early 1970s, adding built-in cost-of-living adjustments (COLA). It wasn't until the late 1970s that things slowed down. During the decades following World War II, while Social Security was ramping up, private pension plans designed to mesh with government programs were expanding. Even with the private pensions, however, it was Social Security that provided the majority of finances for aging Americans.

There may not have been enough money through these programs to provide retirees with everything they ever wanted, but it was enough that many older workers could leave their jobs on their terms (not right before they died).

THE RISE OF AMERICA'S MIDDLE CLASS

A Retired Class Is Born

Yes, Social Security has a historied past, but what are the wider impacts of the program as a whole? In truth, Social Security was vital in creating the American middle class.

It's a bit startling to think that until the mid-twentieth century, the middle class didn't really exist, at least not like it does today. This went hand in hand with the fact that a retired class of people who stood out from the rest of the population didn't really exist either. That began to change, though, due in part to the vision of people like Del Webb.

Webb was the real estate developer who took a radical gamble with the creation of Sun City in Arizona. This was the landmark retirement community based on age segregation—no young people allowed—that became a model with three key characteristics:

- **Activity:** There would be plenty to do.
- **Economy:** Houses would be affordable; costs for common facilities would be spread among all residents.
- **Individuality:** Residents would be free to choose whatever they wanted to do.

The convergence of social policies after World War II helped make life at a Sun City–type of retirement community possible. Postwar, cheap government loans enabled young families to purchase their homes in mass numbers. These homes appreciated in value, creating a worthwhile asset that could be cashed in when going to work and raising the kids had finished. The expanding Social Security program laid the groundwork for predictable income in addition to the tangible asset that homeownership provided.

Social Security in Sweden

Not surprisingly, Sweden, often pointed to as an example of democratic socialism, has a firmly embedded system of government assistance for the elderly. Sweden's old-age pension begins at age sixty-three. Employers' contributions amount to 31.42% of the employee's gross salary. In many instances, government assistance is accompanied by private pensions. If you have a low income (or none) and have lived in Sweden for at least three years, you are entitled to an additional pension. With its extensive provisions for childcare, maternity leave, disability payments, and housing allowances, Sweden provides "cradle to grave" social insurance for its citizens.

At the same time, a shift was occurring in the family structure. In a preindustrial agrarian culture, every person was needed to work the land for as long as possible. Older family members were valued for their knowledge. The family farm was needed for survival, and transferring ownership did not happen until the owner died. The younger family members cared for the aging members. This family ecosystem changed forever when new industries arose, people became more mobile, and they were no longer tied to the land for survival.

Social Security in Canada

Canadians aged sixty-five or older and who have an income of less than $142,609 per year receive payments from the Old Age Security pension (OAS). If they make more than $81,761 per year, when tax time comes the OAS claws back some of that money at a rate of 15% of net income. Canadian citizens and legal residents are eligible for the OAS scheme if they:

- Have lived in Canada for at least ten years from the time they turned eighteen
- Canadian citizens living outside Canada may still qualify if they lived in Canada for at least twenty years after age eighteen

Leisure Time

With people living longer and having the financial flexibility to quit working, the question "What to do?" arose. In the mid-twentieth century, many viewed retirement as a period of leisure. If work was a hard slog, then retirement would be the payoff with nothing to think about other than how to enjoy oneself. The notion of age-segregated communities ignited a positive response because there would be a place for the older members of the population. These communities were seen as a reward for a lifetime of hard work. One thing was clear: There was a very clean line between work and retirement. Work was work, and retirement was fun.

The Search for Something More Than Fun

Frenetic activity in the pursuit of fun hardly seems to define relaxation. The concept of luring a massive portion of the nation's population to reservations of recreation was an artificial design. Although keeping busy has its merits, it has its limits.

Not all seniors were decamping to retirement communities. Some, whether for lack of sufficient financial resources or simply lack of interest, were leaving work and going nowhere. All that experience, talent, and skill were sitting idle, waiting to be released in a meaningful direction. It should come as no surprise that today there is an explosion of new opportunities. Retired folks around the world are blazing paths and opening minds to a new understanding of what a fulfilling after-work life means.

FUNDING SOCIAL SECURITY

Paying It Forward

One of the most common myths about Social Security is that you won't get back the money you put in. This myth persists because the money you pay into the system isn't held in a trust for when you retire; instead, it's used to pay benefits for workers who are retired *right now*.

INVESTING ITS FUNDS

Contrary to popular belief, the money in the Social Security Trust Funds is invested and earns income. Social Security invests in US Treasury bonds, one of the safest investments in the world, as those bonds are backed by the full faith and credit of the United States.

Social Security is also mandatory for US workers. There's no possibility of people suddenly deciding to opt out of it. So, money will always be flowing in to fund retirement and other Social Security benefits.

RUNNING OUT OF MONEY?

Though all of these facts are out there for the public to verify, there are still persistent rumors (louder during an election cycle) that Social Security is running out of money.

It's true that over the years the government has had to make adjustments to ensure that the system continues to have the wherewithal to pay benefits. When Social Security officially began collecting funds in 1937, it taxed just 2% of a worker's earnings; 1% came from the worker's paycheck and 1% was paid by her or his employer. It taxed up to $3,000 in income. Today that tax has risen to 12.4% of a worker's earnings, which is still split evenly between worker and employer, and the income level cap has been increased to $168,600. (Self-employed people pay a tax of 12.4% on their earnings, acting as both the employer and employee.) So over time, Social Security taxes have increased.

Does the Government Raid Social Security?

Some people have charged that Social Security's difficulties, real or imagined, are caused by the government burrowing into its trust funds and spending the money on various other projects. However, this charge misunderstands the fact that these aren't really trust funds. They're government accounts, and the money from them is invested.

The government funds Social Security in three ways:

1. From payroll taxes collected on workers' paychecks. This is the FICA tax.
2. From money deposited in the Social Security Trust Funds, which is invested in Treasury bonds and earns interest. This money represents a surplus collected when taxed income exceeds the amount paid out in benefits.
3. From income tax that beneficiaries with high incomes pay on Social Security benefits.

Overall, the program ran a surplus until 2020. However, the trust funds will likely be depleted sometime in the 2030s (exact dates vary, depending on who's doing the estimating). Even in that case, using payroll taxes and income tax, the program can continue to pay out approximately 80% of benefits if nothing changes. However, as you'll see in the next section, there are a number of ways in which Social Security can be fixed that will make it solvent for a long time to come.

In addition to payroll taxes to fund Social Security, employees and their employers each pay 1.45% tax to fund Medicare Part A. High-income individuals pay an additional 0.9% to support Medicare.

IS SOCIAL SECURITY UNFAIR TO YOUNG PEOPLE?

One popular argument is that Social Security is a burden on the younger generation. When the system was created, the argument goes, there were fifty-five workers to support each retiree, so the payroll tax each worker paid could be kept very low. But since 1935, the life expectancy of the average worker has dramatically increased. The result is that it takes more and more younger workers to support retired older ones. It's been estimated that to continue to function, the system needs approximately 2.8 younger workers for each retiree Social Security supports.

If the ratio slips below the critical level, we will reach a situation in which too few workers must support too many retirees. This is the crisis that doomsayers are warning about. But is the situation as dire as they claim? Let's look at what's really wrong with Social Security and how it can be fixed.

FIXING SOCIAL SECURITY

Countering the Myth of Collapse

Spend any time on the Internet and you'll come across someone claiming that Social Security is on the verge of collapse. Those people assert that the system is overwhelmed. Millions of newly retired baby boomers are filing claims every day. It's only a matter of time before the system runs out of money. It's hard to know if these claims have any truth to them, or whether they're all lies. This entry dives into the questions many have about the shelf life of Social Security.

WILL SOCIAL SECURITY GO BANKRUPT?

From 1985 to 2009, the government took in more money in payroll taxes for Social Security than it paid out in benefits. The resulting surplus went into the Social Security Trust Funds, where it earned interest. However, beginning in 2010, benefits exceeded revenues from payroll taxes. If this trend continues, the trust funds will run out of money by 2037. (Note that this assumes the economy grows at an average rate of 1.7%. A faster average growth could mean the system would remain fully solvent for longer.)

However, this does not mean that the system will be bankrupt by 2037. Social Security is set up so that today's workers are paying the cost of today's retirees. In other words, there is *always* money coming into the system because the American workforce continues to work, and payroll taxes continue to be deducted from their paychecks.

In addition, the system continues to have a revenue stream from wealthy individuals paying income tax on their benefits. The third revenue source, remember, is the interest earned by the surplus that went into the trusts. So, the system can't go bankrupt by simply running out of money.

Reduced Benefits

It is true that unless steps are taken by the government, Social Security will no longer have the funds to pay full benefits to retirees by 2037, or possibly sooner—that is, unless the economy starts experiencing a faster growth rate. At that point, experts estimate that tax revenues would only account for about 76%–80% of full benefits.

Although this is a long way from being bankrupt, it's something no one wants to see happen (especially anyone planning to retire in 2037 or later). More than 55 million baby boomers collect Social Security as of 2024, and that number is expected to increase by 4.1 million annually for the next several years. If the system is going to be able to handle those numbers, the politicians in Washington, DC need to start considering some possible fixes.

Changes in the Past

Change is nothing new to Social Security. Over the years it has seen a number of adjustments, from the amount of payroll taxes deducted to cost-of-living adjustments (COLA). The tax rate first increased in 1950 from 2% to 3%. The following year, the upper limit on taxable income was raised for the first time from $3,000 to $3,600.

HOW COULD SOCIAL
SECURITY BE FIXED?

A number of possible changes to the system have been proposed to extend its solvency and ability to pay full benefits. Some of these are more politically possible than others, and almost all are controversial.

Privatize the System

At the beginning of his second term, President George W. Bush proposed the partial privatization of Social Security. His proposal would have allowed participants in the program to move up to one-third of their payroll tax to personalized investment accounts. The plan was aimed primarily at younger workers; older workers were exempt from it.

Although the plan had the backing of many conservatives, others opposed it, along with virtually all Democratic Party politicians. Bush campaigned energetically for the plan, but ultimately it failed to gain traction.

Many commentators pointed out that after the Great Recession of 2008–2009, privatized accounts could have severely impacted many workers' retirement savings. It seems unlikely in the near future that any politician will be able to privatize Social Security, in part or in whole.

Raise the Earnings Cap or Payroll Tax

Under the present system, payroll taxes for Social Security are not deducted from earnings above $168,600 as of 2024. (As previously mentioned, this cap has been raised a number of times in the program's history; it started out at $3,000.) One relatively simple way to make the program solvent in the future is to raise this cap again. Eliminating the cap would cut the program's shortfall (the amount that couldn't be covered by existing funding).

Another way to increase the amount of money in the system is to hike the payroll tax, which accounts for the large majority of revenue that flows into the system. Remember that this tax began in 1937 at 1% each from both worker and employer and is currently at 6.2% for each of them. It's estimated that if the tax was raised by 1%, to 7.2% for worker and employer, this alone could account for up to 50% of the program's shortfall.

That said, raising taxes is never easy, and it's hard to say whether Congress would have the political fortitude to take either of the steps mentioned. In addition, since lower-earning workers get more of a return on their contributions than higher-earning workers, raising the earnings cap would be unpopular with richer contributors.

Expanding Coverage

Although Social Security covers the overwhelming majority of US workers, some are still outside it. Roughly 25% of state and government workers use a pension system for their retirements rather than paying into Social Security. If the system expanded to cover them as well, it's estimated that this could reduce the program's shortfall by about 6%. However, this would mean higher government contributions to pensions to fully compensate those workers who remain covered by them. For this reason, state and city governments generally oppose such a move.

Cut Benefits

The solutions proposed so far assume that the goal is for the system to continue to pay the same level of benefits. But suppose, instead, the government were to cut benefits. This would certainly help the program remain solvent. That said, beneficiaries would likely be annoyed by this new reality. Such a program would have to be carefully phased in, would have to be graded from lower-earning workers to higher earners, and politically would be immensely unpopular.

Adjust the Cost of Living

In 1975, Congress mandated automatic cost-of-living adjustments within the system. Benefits are currently tied to the Consumer Price Index for Urban Wage Earners and Clerical Workers (CPI-W). Some people have proposed changing this, and instead link benefits to what is called a chained Consumer Price Index (CPI). The chained CPI rises a bit slower than the CPI-W and making this switch would save significant amounts of money in the long run—it would cut the shortfall by about 18%.

The downside to this, of course, is that beneficiaries would receive a lower cost-of-living increase, something that no one would welcome.

Raising the Full Retirement Age (FRA)

Finally, there's the option of increasing the age at which workers can take their full benefits. This book will later explore how your FRA is calculated; for now, just note that in the current system, if you were born in 1960 or later, you reach your FRA at age sixty-seven. (You can take benefits before then, but they'll be less than they would be if you waited until your FRA; more discussion of this later.) The argument has been made that since longevity is increasing, people should expect to work longer and therefore the FRA should be pushed back. Moving the FRA back a single year, to sixty-eight, could reduce the shortfall by up to 23%.

Of course, many people aren't enthusiastic about adding another year of work onto their careers. They want to get as many golden years as possible.

ESTIMATING THE POLITICAL PRICE

All of the solutions mentioned in this section have political costs, and none will, by itself, eliminate Social Security's shortfall. But it's likely that eventually some combination of these changes will be used to keep the program solvent into the next century.

GETTING A SOCIAL SECURITY CARD

Joining the System

When you start your first job, you must have a Social Security number (SSN); you can't be legally hired without it. So, even though you technically aren't required to have an SSN, for all practical purposes you'll need one at some point in your life. As has been pointed out, SSNs have become a basic means of identification for most Americans, precisely because they're so widespread.

HOW EARLY SHOULD YOU GET A CARD?

Many parents take care of the issue of SSNs very early—pretty much when their baby is born. It's easiest to do this when you're giving information to the hospital, which they'll use to generate your child's birth certificate. The Social Security Administration points out that waiting longer can create delays while they work to verify the birth certificate.

Why Does a Baby Need a Social Security Number?

No, your baby isn't going to get a job anytime soon, but there are other reasons for them to have an SSN:

- If you're planning to claim your child as a dependent and take advantage of valuable tax credits
- If you want to open a bank account in your baby's name

- If you're going to buy savings bonds for the child
- If you're getting medical coverage for your offspring
- If you're applying for government services for the child

To apply at a Social Security office, you'll need to bring proof of your baby's age, US citizenship, and identity, as well as proof of your own identity. Then you'll fill out Form SS-5. The SSA will take up to twelve weeks to issue your child a Social Security card. If your child is twelve or older, she or he must be present in person at the SSA office when you fill out the application. Plus, the SSA only accepts certain documents as proof of citizenship, such as:

- US birth certificate
- US Consular Report of Birth Abroad
- US passport
- Certificate of Naturalization
- Certificate of Citizenship

If for some reason you don't have your child's birth certificate, the SSA will accept a US passport; a religious record made before your child turned five that shows the date of birth; or a US hospital record of birth.

Born Abroad

If your child was born abroad, when you apply for their Social Security number, you'll need to bring one of the following:

- Foreign birth certificate
- Certificate of Report of Birth

- Consular Report of Birth Abroad
- Certificate of Naturalization
- Passport

The SSA is also a bit picky about what they will and won't accept as proof of identity—"An acceptable document must be current (not expired) and show your child's name, identifying information, and preferably, a recent photograph." They may also accept:

- State-issued non-driver identification card
- Adoption decree
- Doctor, hospital, or clinic record
- Religious record
- Daycare or school record
- School identification card

APPLYING FOR YOUR OWN SOCIAL SECURITY CARD

Getting a Social Security number for yourself is similar to getting one for your child. To prove your identity, you can show one of the following:

- US driver's license
- State-issued non-driver identification card
- US passport
- Employee identification card

- School identification card
- Health insurance card (*not* Medicaid)
- US military identification card
- Life insurance policy

The SSA will want to see the original documents, so don't bother bringing photocopies; they won't be accepted.

There's no cost for getting a Social Security number and card. On a PDF they distribute, the SSA warns, "If someone contacts you and wants to charge you for getting a number or card, please remember that these Social Security services are free. You can report anyone attempting to charge you by calling our Office of the Inspector General hotline at 1-800-269-0271."

WHAT TO DO IF YOU'RE A NONCITIZEN

Usually, the only noncitizens needing Social Security numbers are those authorized to work in the United States by the Department of Homeland Security. For example, noncitizens who are in the United States on a student visa generally don't need a Social Security card to do many of the things American citizens do—get a driver's license or register for school, for instance.

If you need an SSN, you can apply in your home country before coming to the United States or, having arrived in America, you can visit your local SSA office. The first is the easier option.

When you visit the SSA, you'll need your paperwork showing that you're authorized to work in the United States. The SSA recommends you wait until ten days after arriving in the United States to make your application, since that will give the agency time to verify your documents from the Department of Homeland Security. You'll also need:

- Two documents verifying your identity, immigration status, and age
- A completed application for a Social Security card (Form SS-5), which you can download from the SSA's website

As usual, the documents must be original and not photocopies. Acceptable documents include a passport along with a Machine Readable Immigrant Visa (MRIV) or a Permanent Resident Card (Form I-551) if you have it already. You can't use one document as two forms of identification; the best and easiest forms are your birth certificate and passport.

If you hold a J-1 exchange visa (dependents use J-2 visas), the SSA will want to see your Certificate of Eligibility for Exchange Visitor Status (Form DS-2019). If you're a student holding a J-1 visa, you'll have to provide the SSA with a letter from your sponsor on the sponsor's letterhead, including an original signature. The letter should authorize you to work in the United States.

If you are an international student with an F-1 or M-1 visa, the SSA will need to see your Certificate of Eligibility for Nonimmigrant Student Status (Form I-20).

You'll receive your Social Security card in the mail.

GETTING ANOTHER CARD

Making Changes

Life happens, and things change. A lot of those things, like changing your name or losing your wallet, can lead to the need for a new Social Security card. Depending on the reason for the replacement, you'll need to follow different channels to get it taken care of. In most cases, the easiest option will be to go through your *my* Social Security account to order your new card online. If you haven't set up your account yet, you'll want to do that as soon as possible.

REPLACING OR CHANGING YOUR CARD

Sometimes, your original Social Security card needs to be replaced. Whether that's because your name has changed or because the card was lost or stolen, there are specific steps you need to take for a replacement.

Changing Your Name

If you legally change your name when you get married, divorced, or for some other reason, you will have to change your name on your Social Security card. This is important because the government has to ensure that your earnings are properly tracked to credit your benefits. It would be really bad if, because you neglected to change your name in the SSA's records, five or ten years of your working life was credited to the wrong benefit account. Fortunately, changing your name with the SSA isn't difficult.

If you've recently married and have changed your name, go to an SSA office with the marriage certificate as well as a document proving your previous identity (an expired driver's license will work fine). If you've recently divorced and changed your name, bring a copy of the divorce decree and a document proving your new name.

If you have been adopted or have recently become a naturalized citizen, bring an adoption decree or Certificate of Naturalization. You should also bring two documents identifying you by your old name and by your new name.

Lost or Stolen Card

If your card disappears it's *extremely important* that you report the loss and get a replacement card as soon as possible. Identity theft is among the most widespread crimes being practiced today, and as mentioned earlier, Social Security numbers are widely used as a form of identification. You're only allowed to replace it three times in the course of a year and can only have ten replacement cards over your lifetime.

In some cases, you'll be able to apply for your replacement card online through your *my* Social Security account (more on that in a moment). You can use this quick and easy option if you:

- Are a US citizen eighteen years or older, with a US mailing address
- Are *only* requesting a replacement card (not a name change)
- Have a valid driver's license or state-issued ID card from one of the following:
  - District of Columbia (driver's license only)
  - Iowa
  - Kentucky
  - Michigan
  - Nebraska
  - New Mexico
  - Washington
  - Wisconsin (driver's license only)

If you think someone is fraudulently using your card or your child's card, there are several ways to report it:

- Go to www.idtheft.gov
- Call 1-877-438-4338; or TTY: 1-866-653-4261

MY SOCIAL SECURITY

The Social Security Administration created a website called *my* Social Security (www.ssa.gov/myaccount) to make your life easier. The site will guide you through the steps you need to take to set up your account. Then you can use it to do a wide variety of tasks such as: check the status if you've applied for a card, request a replacement card, review your earnings record, find out your estimated retirement benefits, secure proof that you're not currently receiving benefits, get a benefit verification letter if you are receiving benefits, create or change direct deposit for your benefits, get a copy of your Social Security benefits tax form (Form SSA-1099), or change your address.

Using your online portal can be much easier, quicker, and less stressful than visiting a Social Security office to get these tasks managed.

Setting Up Your Account

If you're a US citizen over eighteen with a Social Security number and an email address, you can set up your *my* Social Security account online. Creating your account requires having set up credentials with either Login.gov or ID.me, two service providers that verify identity as part of the sign-up process.

Your first step is to visit www.ssa.gov/myaccount and click on "Create an Account." If you already have an ID.me or Login.gov account, you'll be able to access your *my* Social Security account right away. If not, you can do it right from this site by choosing either "Create an account with Login.gov" or "Sign in with ID.me." That will kick off your one-time identity verification process. The Login.gov process requires a one-time activation code to finish setting up your *my* Social Security account. Once all of this is done, you'll have full access to your *my* Social Security account.

Verify Your Earnings Record

Your Social Security benefits will be based on your lifetime earnings. If your earnings record is wrong, which is more common than you'd expect, you may not get all the benefits you deserve. That's why you'll want to review your earnings record and make sure that it's correct.

Log on to your *my* Social Security account and navigate to your earnings record. This will be a complete listing of your qualifying income for every year you paid into the Social Security system.

Match up their records with yours to make sure that what's appearing in your record is correct and includes every year you've worked. If you've worked multiple jobs or had a job and self-employment income in the same year, those amounts will be combined in your earnings record. Your current year earnings may be off, as it takes time for the administration to process all the information they receive. But if you see an error for an earlier year, you'll want to address that right away. Generally, you have a little over three years to report mistakes for a specific tax year, but you may be able to get a correction for an earlier year as well.

You can report errors and request corrections by calling Social Security at 1-800-772-1213. Make sure to have any supporting documents, like Form W-2 or Form 1040, readily available.

PROTECTING YOUR SOCIAL SECURITY NUMBER

Guard Against Identity Theft

SSNs are among the most widely used forms of identification in the United States. You use them to get everything from a driver's license to a credit card. For that reason, protecting your SSN is extremely important. If you don't protect your SSN carefully enough (or if you simply have bad luck), you may be subjected to identity theft.

IDENTITY THEFT IN THE UNITED STATES

Particularly with the expansion of the Internet and the growth of sophisticated computer systems, identity theft in the United States has skyrocketed. The Federal Trade Commission (FTC) reported more than 1.1 million identity theft complaints in 2022, with new credit card account fraud making up nearly half. This is largely due to an alarming increase in data breaches since 2016, with more than 1,800 breaches reported in 2022 alone, affecting 422.1 million individuals.

Students and Identity Theft

Many college students are victims of identity theft, partly because they are at the age when they start to obtain credit cards. Also, the practice of universities posting student grades by SSNs is one way in which a student's identity is often stolen. This gives thieves a list of valid SSNs they can exploit.

All of these statistics suggest the importance of protecting your identity, particularly your SSN. The SSA and other organizations have many suggestions about the best ways to do this. Here are a few:

Don't Carry Your Social Security Card with You

There's no reason at all for you to carry your Social Security card around in your wallet. It can be stolen, you could lose your wallet, or you might leave it somewhere. Your Social Security card is extremely important, and you should not treat it carelessly.

Leave it at home, preferably somewhere safe where you keep other important documents. To keep it really safe, rent a safe-deposit box at your bank and store it there.

Don't Give Out Your SSN Unless You Have To

There are a relatively limited number of circumstances in which you will have to provide your Social Security number to anyone. If you open a bank account or apply for a credit card, you'll be asked to provide it. But there's no reason for most people to know it. It's not uncommon for various retailers to ask for the last four digits of your SSN, but be cautious about giving out the full number.

The Bank Scam

This is a widespread scam that particularly targets elderly people. Someone calls you, saying they're from the bank. The caller informs you that there's been some questionable activity in your account. So far, this all sounds normal. This kind of thing happens, and usually the bank will (assuming the suspicious transactions are unauthorized) void your debit/credit card and issue you a new one. But this time, the friendly voice on the other end of the line asks you to "confirm" your account with your SSN and your bank account number. This is fraudulent, and your bank would not call asking for these details.

Beware of Unsecured Websites

A huge amount (though not all) of identity theft takes place through the Internet as cybersecurity threats increase. All of us are so connected—through our smartphones, laptops, tablets, and other devices—that we tend to grow careless about protecting important information like our Social Security numbers.

If a website address begins with https:// (as opposed to http://; the letter *s* is the key here), that indicates that it's a secured site. You should still be cautious about giving out your SSN, but at least on a secured site you will be relatively safe from identity theft.

In general, don't click on websites unless you are confident that they're legitimate. Many scammers set up websites that look as if they are real banks, motor vehicle agencies, and other similar sites.

The same thing goes for email. If you receive an email from someone you don't know or an unexpected email from someone you do know, delete it rather than open it. If you do open it, do not click on any links. If you're concerned that it might be a legitimate issue, go directly to the appropriate website or contact the business like you normally would rather than clicking any links. Many such emails are designed to steal your personal information, including your SSN, and they can look exactly like emails from your bank and other companies you do business with.

Get a Shredder

Identity thieves look for documents that contain your SSN. With all the letters that come in the mail for you, it's not surprising that some of it will have information that identity thieves find valuable. You can deny them access to this sort of information by running your billing receipts, credit card offers, and other documents through a shredder. Shredders are cheap, and you can pick one up at your local office supplies store.

Phishing, Smishing, and Vishing for Numbers

An extremely common online scam technique is called "phishing." Here's how it works: You receive a piece of unsolicited email. It might appear to come from someone you know (your bank, for instance), or it might be an enticement that offers you something for nothing ("Click here for thousands of dollars in free quality merchandise!"). If you click on the link and go to the site, you'll be asked to put in various bits of information—your password, your SSN, your address, and so on. The owners of the site want you to give them as much information as possible so they can steal your identity. A good rule of thumb is to be suspicious of unsolicited emails and avoid sites with which you're not familiar. And be wary of great offers. If something sounds too good to be true, it probably is.

Along with phishing, many scammers have added smishing and vishing to their repertoires. These work similarly to phishing, but they use different contact methods. Smishing uses text messaging to trick people into clicking links, sharing personal and financial information, and downloading damaging apps. In fact, the FTC reports that impersonating banks is the most common texting scam, costing consumers around $330 million in 2022. Vishing, or voice phishing, involves phone calls that look like they're coming from companies you do business with, especially banks and credit card companies. They spoof the actual phone number to appear legit and end up stealing personal information.

Social Media Scams

Social media is the newest arena for identity theft scams. According to the FTC, social media–related online shopping scams are among the most commonly reported. These scams, where people order products on platforms like Facebook or Instagram but never get them, have cost consumers approximately $2.7 billion since 2021.

WHAT TO DO

If, despite your best precautions, you think your SSN has been stolen, then you need to take immediate action to prevent serious damage from happening to your accounts and your credit. You should:

- File a police report as soon as you discover the theft. Sadly, identity theft has become extremely common, so police resources are stretched. There is a limited amount the police can do to help you. But you should still notify them to help protect yourself in the event that someone attempts to use your identity.
- Get in touch with the fraud department at all banks, credit card companies, and other financial institutions where you have accounts. Inform them that someone has stolen your SSN. They'll take steps to monitor your account for suspicious activity. They will likely issue you new debit and credit cards.
- Report the theft to the three major credit score agencies: Equifax, TransUnion, and Experian. Ask them to place a fraud alert and a credit freeze in your file.
- Contact the Internal Revenue Service at www.irs.gov/uac/identity-protection or call them at 1-800-829-1040.
- Get in touch with the Federal Trade Commission at www.idtheft.gov. You can also call 1-877-IDTHEFT (1-877-438-4338).

Once you've reported the theft, you can start damage control. Start by closing any new accounts opened in your name (that you didn't open). Make corrections to your credit report. Request that financial institutions remove any bogus transactions from your accounts.

After doing this, carefully monitor your bank account and credit card accounts. Keep up the monitoring for several months to make sure there's no unauthorized activity. If there is, report it immediately to your bank and the appropriate credit card companies.

Myths about Social Security Numbers

The tinfoil hat crowd on the Internet has spread some strange rumors over the years about SSNs. Among these is the idea that your SSN contains information that identifies you to the government. In particular, it's said that the middle two numbers indicate your race. This is untrue. The first three digits are an area number; the second two are a group number; and the last four are a serial number. There are no hidden codes or meanings in any of this.

Your SSN is deeply important to maintaining your identity as a US citizen. Never be careless with it.

QUALIFICATIONS FOR RECEIVING BENEFITS

Who's Eligible?

A lot of myths have been passed around the Internet about who's receiving Social Security benefits. Some suggest that there is massive fraud in the system and that people are getting two, three, or more sets of benefit payments.

While there's unquestionably some degree of fraud practiced in relation to the system (like any large, complex system, Social Security is subject to some degree of fraud), the truth is that the retirement part of Social Security works pretty much the way it's supposed to. Those who paid into the system are the ones who get benefits. Those who didn't, don't.

All US citizens who work in the United States are qualified to receive Social Security benefits. As a worker, every time you receive a paycheck, money gets deducted from it to pay for the Social Security system. As mentioned earlier, these deductions, or payroll tax, are marked on your check as FICA, which stands for Federal Insurance Contributions Act.

As it's currently set up, Social Security gives you one credit for every $1,730 you earn. You can earn a maximum of four credits per year, and when you've earned forty credits, you're eligible to start receiving benefits. (Keep in mind that the $1,730 number is adjusted each year to take inflation and other things into account.)

WHO ELSE QUALIFIES?

Assuming you fall into the category of those qualifying for benefits, there are some members of your family who may also be eligible to receive benefits. These include:

- Your spouse, if she or he is sixty-two or older
- Your spouse, if she or he cares for a dependent child who is younger than sixteen or is disabled
- Your children, if you're collecting benefits. The children must be either:
  - Younger than eighteen and not married
  - Disabled
  - Full-time students up to and including the age of nineteen and unmarried
- Dependent grandchildren
- An ex-spouse who is at least sixty-two and retired, hasn't remarried, and to whom you were married at least ten years and have been divorced from for at least two years

Expanding the Definition of Marriage

Like other agencies of the federal government, the Social Security Administration adapted to changing definitions of marriage. For example, the SSA recognizes same-sex marriage as qualifying for spousal benefits throughout all fifty states.

When a Breadwinner Dies

There are certain circumstances in which someone can receive Social Security benefits even if he or she isn't yet sixty-two years old. For example, if a family's principal breadwinner dies, then the widow or widower might be eligible to receive Social Security benefits. This will be discussed more thoroughly in a later section of this book. For now, just note that this is an aspect of coverage within the Social Security system.

HOW MUCH WILL YOU GET?

In determining the amount of money to pay a beneficiary, the SSA takes three key factors into account:

1. How long you have worked
2. How much you earned
3. How old you are when you decide to start taking benefits

These determinations apply whether you've spent your career being employed by other people or if you have been self-employed for all or part of your working life.

Your Working Life

The Social Security Administration reviews the totality of your working life, specifically focusing on your top-earning thirty-five years. Note that these years do not need to be consecutive. If you had significant earnings for ten years and then were unemployed for a couple of years, and you then worked again for another twenty-five years, the government will discount the unemployed years.

Who Doesn't Qualify?

Even though most US workers are covered by Social Security, some are not. These include:

- Federal workers who were hired before 1984
- Some state and local workers
- Railroad workers who've worked on the railroads for more than ten years

  But that still leaves more than 95% of the US workforce covered.

If you didn't work for an entire thirty-five years, the SSA will fill in the empty years with zeros. This is one reason why it's a good idea to keep working for as long as possible, especially if your employment over the years has been a bit spotty.

The years don't have to be those that you worked most recently. The SSA starts from the beginning of your working life—when you first started paying taxes into the system—and goes from there.

Using these top thirty-five years of your career, the SSA creates an average called the average indexed monthly earnings (AIME). They use this number to determine your primary insurance amount (PIA), which is what your monthly benefit will be once you've reached your FRA. All of this information is encapsulated in your Social Security statement, which will be discussed in more detail later in this book.

Immigrants

The Social Security Administration reaches out to immigrants in a number of ways:

- By visiting www.ssa.gov/multilanguage, immigrants who do not know English well can choose from eighteen other languages to read about Social Security.
- Immigrants can request the services of an interpreter, whom the SSA will provide, free of charge.

If you are a foreign student holding an F-1, J-1, or M-1 visa and are working on campus or by a special arrangement with the college or university, your earnings will not be taxed for purposes of Social Security. However, if you have a work visa of a different type, your wages can be taxed for Social Security. For more information about this, go to www.irs.gov/forms-pubs and look for publications 515 and 519. You can also call the Internal Revenue Service directly at 1-800-829-1040.

Your Starting Date

Another important factor that affects the amount of your monthly benefit is when you decide to start taking those benefits.

The earliest age at which you can apply for Social Security benefits is sixty-two. However, this isn't necessarily when you *should* start collecting them. This will be explained later in more detail; for now, mark age sixty-two as the date you can first start collecting your benefits.

Of course, if you continue working, especially if you have a reasonably high-earning job, you increase the earnings used to calculate your AIME and thus, potentially, raise the amount of your benefit. This situation lasts until you reach age seventy. At that point, your AIME is fixed. You can continue to work, of course, but it won't have any effect on increasing your benefit.

YOUR FULL RETIREMENT AGE

When You're Expected to Retire

Although you can start taking your benefits at age sixty-two, it's usually better to wait until you reach what the Social Security Administration calls your full retirement age (FRA). If you wait until then, you'll receive your full retirement benefit, although you can increase the amount of your benefit even more by waiting until age seventy to file a claim.

DETERMINING YOUR FRA

Congress changed the FRA in 1983. Up to that point, it had been pinned at age sixty-five. This was the age at which it was anticipated that baby boomers would start to retire in large numbers (and thus start claiming benefits). Congress took several steps to increase the amount of money Social Security was taking in. One step was to increase the payroll tax rate. Another step was to increase the FRA.

The following table indicates how the SSA currently determines full retirement age.

YEAR OF BIRTH	FRA
1954	66 years
1955	66 years 2 months
1956	66 years 4 months
1957	66 years 6 months
1958	66 years 8 months
1959	66 years 10 months
1960 and after	67 years

FIGURING OUT YOUR LIFE EXPECTANCY

When you're trying to determine when you should begin taking Social Security benefits, the underlying unknown is: How much longer are you going to be alive? Obviously, it's impossible to predict the answer to that with any degree of certainty, but statisticians have given us a pretty good general idea. Their conclusions are reflected in the following table.

AGE	MALE TOTAL YEARS REMAINING	FEMALE TOTAL YEARS REMAINING
0	74.1	79.8
1	73.6	79.2
5	69.6	75.2
10	64.7	70.2
15	59.7	65.3
20	55.0	60.4
25	50.4	55.6
30	45.9	50.8
35	41.4	46.1
40	37.0	41.4
45	32.6	36.8
50	28.3	32.2
55	24.2	27.9
60	20.5	23.7
65	16.9	19.7
70	13.6	15.8
75	10.5	12.3

80	7.7	9.1
85	5.5	6.4
90	3.7	4.4
95	2.6	3.1
100	1.9	2.2
105	1.5	1.6

Clearly there are lots of factors involved, and this chart is pretty simple. For a more sophisticated and complex calculation, you can try the life expectancy calculator at sites like www.livingto100.com and www.longevityillustrator.org.

The purpose of this examination is to help you figure out whether or not you should take early benefits—that is, start collecting them before you reach your FRA. In general, you're trying to determine what financial planners call a "break-even point." You do this by comparing the differing amounts you'll get from Social Security depending on when you claim benefits and how long you live after that. If you claim benefits early but don't live to your break-even age, then you made the right decision to claim early. If you claim later and live longer, you again made the right decision, since your benefit will be larger than if you'd claimed early. The unfortunate decision is to claim early and then live up to or past your break-even age. That's the point at which you may have financial difficulties because of the smaller size of your benefit and the resulting smaller cost-of-living increases. Subsequent sections will discuss the advantages (and disadvantages) of taking early benefits versus claiming later.

GETTING STARTED WITH SOCIAL SECURITY

What You Need to Know

Although it's pretty easy to apply for benefits, the Social Security Administration recommends that you apply three months before you want your benefits to start coming. They strongly urge you to apply online rather than in person.

"In most cases, once your application is submitted electronically, you're done. There are no forms to sign and usually no documentation is required. Social Security will process your application and contact you if any further information is needed."

—Social Security Administration

You can use the online application if you're at least sixty-one years and nine months old, are not currently receiving benefits, haven't already applied for benefits (say, at a regional SSA office), and don't want benefits to start any later than four months from the time you apply.

You can apply online on the Social Security Administration's website, www.ssa.gov/onlineservices. The SSA's online hours of operation are Monday through Friday 4:15 a.m. to 1:00 a.m. ET; Saturday from 5:00 a.m. to 11:00 p.m. ET; and Sunday from 8:00 a.m. to 11:30 p.m. ET.

OTHER WAYS TO APPLY

There are two other ways to apply for benefits: over the phone and in person.

Applying in Person

Sitting around and waiting at the SSA office can take some time. However, you can significantly cut down on your wait time by making an appointment ahead of time. Call 1-800-772-1213 and set up a time to talk to someone. Particularly if you're unsure or insecure about parts of the process, this is a good route to go.

Applying over the Phone

To apply over the phone, call 1-800-772-1213 Monday through Friday between 8:00 a.m. and 7:00 p.m. However, be aware that the phone lines are likely to be busy early in the morning and will be especially busy early in the week and the month. So be ready to sit on hold for quite a while.

WHAT SHOULD YOU KNOW?

Before applying online, over the phone, or in person, you should know the following:

1. **Your full retirement age.** You can learn this from the table in the previous section. Generally speaking, it will be between sixty-six and sixty-seven. You need to know this even if you're applying for benefits before reaching your FRA.

2. **When you can start receiving benefits.** You can start taking benefits any time after turning sixty-two or as late as age seventy. Remember that if you take early benefits (that is, you take them before reaching your FRA), you will not receive your full benefits. If you wait until you reach age seventy, your benefits will be larger than if you start taking them at your FRA.

3. **How working during retirement can affect your benefits.** This will be discussed shortly.

4. **Delayed retirement credits.** This will be explored in the following pages.

5. **Your life expectancy.** Look this up on the table in the previous section.

Retirement Estimator

The Social Security Administration has very kindly provided a Retirement Estimator to calculate how much your benefits will be at different ages. You can access the Retirement Estimator at www.ssa.gov/benefits/calculators/.

Delayed Retirement Credits

If you choose to begin taking your Social Security benefits after you've reached and passed your full retirement age, your benefits increase. The longer you delay, the greater the increase, until you reach age seventy. At that point, the additional increases stop. You can continue to work, of course, but it won't make a difference in the size of your benefits.

The following table, taken from the SSA's website, shows the rate of increase for people born in different years. If you were born January 1, refer to the rate of increase for the previous year.

INCREASE FOR DELAYED RETIREMENT		
Year of Birth	Yearly Rate of Increase	Monthly Rate of Increase
1933–1934	5.5%	11/24 of 1%
1935–1936	6.0%	1/2 of 1%
1937–1938	6.5%	13/24 of 1%
1939–1940	7.0%	7/12 of 1%
1941–1942	7.5%	5/8 of 1%
1943 or later	8.0%	2/3 of 1%

Retroactive Benefits

Here's an important note from the SSA: "If you've already reached full retirement age, you can choose to start receiving benefits before the month you apply. However, we cannot pay retroactive benefits for any month before you reached full retirement age or more than six months in the past."

This is particularly useful if you're past your FRA but have an urgent need for a lump sum of cash, perhaps for a medical emergency. For example, David has decided that rather than beginning his benefits at age sixty-seven, his FRA, he will delay taking them until he reaches age seventy. However, at age sixty-nine he develops an illness that requires a lengthy operation. Not all the cost will be covered by his insurance, so he decides to apply for retroactive Social Security benefits. David receives a delayed retirement credit (DRC) for the two years he's past his FRA. Unfortunately, he can only receive six months' worth of benefits, but all the same the lump sum he receives goes a long way toward paying some of the bills for his operation.

THE DOCUMENTS YOU'LL NEED

To file for Social Security benefits, you have to have a sizable amount of information about yourself, backed up with original documents. The part about "original" is important; the SSA will *not* accept photocopies of your birth certificate and other documentation.

Lost Your Birth Certificate?

If you've lost your birth certificate or never had a copy of it in the first place, the state and city of your birth will be able to provide it to you. Go to city hall in the city or town in which you were born and ask for a copy. You'll have to provide photo ID (your driver's license is sufficient) and pay a small fee to cover the costs of the transaction.

These are the documents you'll need:

- Birth certificate or other proof of birth
- Proof of US citizenship (if you're an alien legally residing in the United States, proof of your legal status)
- If you're a veteran who served before 1968, a copy of your military service papers
- Copies of your W-2 forms (if you work for more than one employer, W-2s from each of them)
- If you're self-employed, a copy of your most recent tax return
- If you're married to the chief breadwinner in the household, your marriage certificate

ESTIMATING YOUR BENEFITS

How Much Are You Going to Get?

You need to take Social Security benefits into account as an important part of your financial picture for retirement. When you begin to draw up your retirement budget, though, you need a clearer idea of exactly how much those benefits might be.

The two factors that determine this are:

1. How much have you earned?
2. When do you intend to start taking benefits?

The first step in determining what the answer to those questions might be comes in the form of your Social Security statement.

YOUR STATEMENT

The Social Security Administration updates your statement annually and makes it available online through your *my* Social Security account. If you don't have that set up, the SSA will mail you a paper statement three months before you turn age sixty.

The Check Is *Not* in the Mail

One significant change from past practices is that the SSA no longer mails out actual physical checks every month to those taking benefits. Since 2011, the SSA has required that recipients of benefits receive their money through electronic transfer to their bank accounts. Therefore, when you sign up for Social Security benefits, you'll have to provide some information about your bank account (specifically, the routing number, which you can find on the bottom left-hand corner of your checks or through your banking app). If you don't have a bank account or don't want to give the SSA information about it, you have the option of using a prepaid debit card. Each month, the amount of your benefits is automatically loaded on the card, and you use it to make purchases, just as you would a regular bank debit card.

What's on Your Statement?

Your statement will contain three things:

1. Your estimated benefits at different retirement ages (in handy graph format)
2. Your year-by-year earnings that the system used to estimate your benefits
3. An explanation of how the SSA uses the information it has gathered to calculate your benefits

Estimated Benefits

In the top right-hand corner of the first page of the statement is your estimated benefits at every age from sixty-two to seventy. Inside, the statement tells you:

- Whether you've earned enough credits to qualify for retirement benefits
- Whether you've earned enough credits to qualify for disability benefits and, if you are disabled right now, what your monthly benefit would be
- Whether your spouse and children would qualify for survivors benefits in the event of your death, and what those monthly

benefits would be (this is broken down by child and spouse caring for the child, as well as spouse if she or he started taking those benefits at your FRA)

- The limit on total family survivors benefits
- Whether you have enough credits to qualify for Medicare

Let's look, briefly, at the statement of Marilyn, who turned sixty-two several months ago. She examines her statement and sees that she's earned enough credits to take Social Security benefits. She can get $1,465 a month if she claims her benefits now. However, if she waits five years until her full retirement age of sixty-seven, her benefits increase to $2,119 per month (an increase of around 45%). Further, if she can wait until she turns seventy to claim, her benefits rise to $2,634, an increase of 24% over the amount she would get by claiming at her FRA, and an increase of almost 80% over what she would get by claiming now. Because she can, Marilyn decides to wait at least until she reaches her FRA. At that point, she can reevaluate the situation and see if she wants to wait until age seventy. (This, of course, is where the issue of life expectancy kicks in. If Marilyn's family has a history of living many years, it makes sense to wait a longer time. If they tend to die earlier, she may want to put in her claim at her FRA or even, depending on her life expectancy, at the early age of sixty-two.)

Year-by-Year Earnings Record

The Year-by-Year Earnings Record is a table on your statement. It shows how much taxable income you earned for each of the thirty-five years that Social Security averaged to come up with your estimated benefits. You may notice that some years are marked with zeros. Those were years in which you had no taxable income. The longer you work, the more of those zeros will go away and be replaced by income numbers, and the higher your estimated benefits will be.

If you earned more than the annual earnings cap ($168,600 for 2024) in a given year, that's all the taxable income the statement will show (even though you may have actually earned quite a bit more). That's because the annual earnings cap is the upper limit on income taxable for Social Security. The totals of tax paid by you and your employer toward Social Security and Medicare are at the bottom of the table.

Marilyn's work history shows considerable variation in her taxable income. For seven years she had none, so these years appear as zero. On the other hand, in one year her taxable income rose to more than $80,000. For the past few years, her taxable income has remained relatively steady. Marilyn knows that her situation will be improved if she can replace those zeros with some numbers. Working past her FRA until she turns seventy will do that, giving her an increased benefit.

Medicare Cap versus Social Security Cap

Although there is a cap on Social Security taxable earnings ($168,600 for 2024), that is not true of Medicare. The maximum taxable amount for Medicare began increasing in 1991, and since 1994 there has been no cap on earnings that are taxable to pay for the program.

Explanation of Social Security
The third part of your statement explains in some detail how your Social Security benefits work. Topics it contains include:

- Cost-of-living adjustments (COLA)
- That these benefits are not intended to be your sole source of income in retirement
- Family benefits
- Spousal benefits

If you're viewing your statement online, this section will also include some important links to resources for assistance and information.

my Social Security

If you want to look at your statement or get other information about your benefits, the best thing is to set up a *my* Social Security account. To set it up, go to www.ssa.gov/myaccount. The site will allow you to access your statement any time you want.

If you find an error in your statement, it's important to notify the SSA immediately so that it can be corrected. If you feel your earnings were misreported for a particular year, find your W-2 or Schedule C for that year and have it in hand when you call the SSA at 1-800-772-1213.

DISABILITY BENEFITS

When You Can't Work Anymore

Disability is something that is difficult, if not impossible, to plan for accurately. You don't know if or when it's going to happen and what sort of financial assistance you'll need. And the fact is, it's more common than you tend to think. It's estimated that a twenty-year-old worker has a one-in-four chance of becoming disabled before she or he reaches full retirement age. The Social Security Administration's statistics show that in 2022 the agency received 1.8 million applications for disability benefits; of those, the SSA awarded benefits in more than 543,000 cases. Currently about 7.4 million workers receive disability payments.

Like other aspects of your financial planning, Social Security is not the sole answer to the financial issues of being unable to work. Nonetheless, Social Security disability benefits can be a big help in coping with something that's personally and professionally devastating.

SOCIAL SECURITY DISABILITY INSURANCE

The government pays two kinds of disability benefits: Social Security Disability Insurance (SSDI) and Supplemental Security Income (SSI). SSI will be discussed in a separate section; Social Security's plans for children who suffer from disabilities will also be examined later. For now, let's concentrate on SSDI.

The SSA explains its disabilities program in this way:

Social Security pays benefits to people who can't work because they have a medical condition that's expected to last at least one year or result in death. While some programs give money to people with partial disability or short-term disability, Social Security does not.

Earnings Tests

To determine whether you're eligible for Social Security disability benefits, you must consider two earnings tests:

1. A recent work test
2. A duration of work test

For the recent work test, the SSA offers the following table:

RULES FOR WORK NEEDED FOR THE RECENT WORK TEST	
IF YOU BECAME DISABLED:	THEN, YOU GENERALLY NEED:
In or before the quarter you turned twenty-four	One and a half years of work during the three-year period ending with the quarter your disability began.
In the quarter after you turned age twenty-four but before the quarter you turned thirty-one	Work during half the time for the period beginning with the quarter after you turned twenty-one and ending with the quarter you became disabled. Example: If you became disabled in the quarter you turned age twenty-seven, then you would need three years of work out of the six-year period ending with the quarter you became disabled.
In the quarter you turned age thirty-one or later	Work during five years out of the ten-year period ending with the quarter your disability began.

The SSA also provides a table to determine where you stand on the work test:

EXAMPLES OF WORK NEEDED FOR THE DURATION OF WORK TEST	
IF YOU BECOME DISABLED:	THEN YOU GENERALLY NEED:
Before age 28	1.5 years of work
Age 30	2 years
Age 34	3 years
Age 38	4 years
Age 42	5 years
Age 44	5.5 years
Age 46	6 years
Age 48	6.5 years
Age 50	7 years
Age 52	7.5 years
Age 54	8 years
Age 56	8.5 years
Age 58	9 years
Age 60	9.5 years

APPLYING FOR DISABILITY BENEFITS

You can apply for disability benefits the same three ways as you can for retirement benefits: by phone, in person, or online. SSDI comes with a five-month waiting period (unless you have been diagnosed with ALS), meaning benefits will start during your sixth full month of being disabled. Plus, the SSA warns that processing time for an application can take anywhere from three to five months, so it's important to start the application process as soon as you're able. To apply, you'll need a lot of information and documentation, including:

- Social Security number
- Birth certificate
- Name, Social Security number, and birth date of your current or former spouse, marriage date and location, and divorce or death date if applicable
- Names, addresses, and phone numbers of the medical personnel who took care of you and the dates on which you received care
- Names and dosages of prescription medicine you take and who prescribed them
- Medical records related to the treatment you're receiving from doctors, therapists, hospitals, and clinics
- Laboratory and test results and the name of the practitioner who ordered them
- The amount of money you earned this year and last year
- Proof of where you worked and what kind of work you did
- A recent W-2 (if self-employed, your most recent tax return)

Sadly, this being the government after all, you'll spend quite a lot of time filling out forms. Keep going, though. This is very important to your financial well-being.

Disability Starter Kit

The SSA has created a Disability Starter Kit to help people prepare for their online application or disability interview. The kit contains a wealth of information about the documents you'll need to submit, the disability programs that may be available to you, and details about their decision-making process.

Deciding If You're Really Disabled

After you've completed your application, it goes to the Disability Determination Services (DDS) in your state for consideration. These folks will contact your doctors or other caregivers to find out more details of your medical condition. It's possible you may have to go for a special examination, either by your doctor or one picked by the DDS. In the end, the DDS makes its recommendation to the SSA about whether to grant your application based on five questions:

1. Are you working?
2. Is your medical condition severe (according to SSA guidelines)?
3. Does your condition match an SSA listing for disability?
4. Can you do the type of work you did before?
5. Can you do any other kind of work based on your age, education, and work experience?

This last point is crucial and is a reason many disability claims are disallowed. Even if you're unable to perform the kind of work you did before you suffered the disability, it's possible you may have the education, training, or physical skills to do something else. If that's the case, your claim will probably be denied.

The SSA will notify you by letter of the resolution of your claim. If the claim's been approved, the letter will tell you how much money you'll get per month and when payments will start.

Appealing a Denial

If your claim is denied and you disagree with the reason (outlined in the letter from the SSA), you have the right to appeal the decision. Appealing a decision by the SSA for the denial of SSDI benefits is the same as any other SSA appeals process. There are further details a bit later how the SSA appeals process works.

FAMILY DISABILITY BENEFITS

Because the government understands that your disability also affects your family members, it's possible to obtain benefits for them as well. These include:

- Your spouse, if she or he is sixty-two or older
- Your spouse, if she or he is caring for your child and the child is younger than sixteen or disabled
- Your unmarried disabled child younger than eighteen
- Your child eighteen or older if she or he has a disability that began before the child reached the age of twenty-two

Other Benefits and Disability

It's possible for other benefits to be affected by your disability benefits. This will be discussed in more detail in the respective sections that cover the Windfall Elimination Provision and the Government Pension Offset.

TICKET TO WORK

If you're eighteen through sixty-four years of age and qualify for disability benefits, the Social Security Administration offers you a program called Ticket to Work. Its object is to train you, free of cost, in skills that can lead to employment and offer services and support to help you succeed. The SSA explains that when you take part in the Ticket to Work program, you can get help finding a job, vocational rehabilitation, or other support. Employment networks and state vocational rehabilitation agencies provide these services. These networks include private organizations and government agencies that have agreed to work with Social Security. They provide employment services and other support to beneficiaries with disabilities.

The key goal of the program is to move people toward self-sufficiency to reduce their reliance on SSDI benefits. The agency offers work incentives that allow participants to continue to receive cash benefits while looking for the right job; if you can't find suitable work, you can return to full benefits. If you want to apply to participate in the program, you can call the Ticket to Work helpline at 1-866-968-7842 or visit the website at www.ssa.gov/work.

SUPPLEMENTAL SECURITY INCOME

Adding to Your Disability Benefits

As you can see from the previous section, the Social Security Administration is careful in its definition of both "disabilities" and who qualifies for disability benefits. These benefits are the primary way in which the system assists workers who, for one reason or another, are unable to work. In this section, you'll learn about a second kind of disability benefit: Supplemental Security Income (SSI).

WHERE DID IT COME FROM?

The original 1935 Social Security Act also mandated three state programs: Aid to the Blind, Old-Age Assistance, and Aid to Dependent Children. In 1950, an amendment was created to include Aid to the Permanently and Totally Disabled. In the 1970s, the Nixon administration decided to federalize and centralize these programs under the umbrella of the SSA. The result was a 1972 amendment creating SSI. The program began paying out benefits in 1974.

Funded Differently

Unlike Social Security, which is primarily funded by a payroll tax (FICA), the SSI is funded out of general Treasury revenues, which come from income tax, corporate taxes, and other sources.

As of November 2023, SSI benefits were going to 7.4 million people, nearly 1 million of whom were under the age of eighteen. These numbers, and the amount of dollars being doled out by the program, go up and down, but generally increase over time. This represents a challenge to the government, since SSI isn't funded the same way as Social Security and therefore isn't subject to the same kinds of fixes that could keep Social Security retirement benefits flowing.

WHO'S ELIGIBLE?

The key determinants for whether or not you qualify for SSI are your age and your income. In calculating your income, the Social Security Administration does *not* count the following:

- The first $20 in income you receive each month from all sources
- The first $65 you earn in a month as wages and half of your earnings over $65 received in a month
- State SSI supplement payments
- Section 8 housing vouchers
- Supplemental Nutrition Assistance Program (SNAP) benefits
- Rent rebates or property tax refunds
- Temporary Assistance for Needy Families (TANF)
- Most home energy assistance

Part of your spouse's income is included in the calculation; if you're under eighteen, the SSA uses part of your parents' income in calculating your income. To qualify for SSI benefits, your income must be less than $943 per month if you're an individual or $1,415 if you're a married couple, though some states (such as California,

Hawaii, and Maryland) may have higher income limits. Note that these figures are as of 2024 and change from year to year. For the latest information on this, go to www.ssa.gov/ssi.

Disabled but Working

If you are disabled but are still working, any money you spend on items you need because you're disabled (for example, a wheelchair, crutches, special transportation) is deducted from the SSA's calculation of your income. Under the same logic, the SSA deducts from the income calculation any money a blind person uses to do their work.

In addition to income, the SSA includes in its means test your resources (that is, assets you own, as opposed to money you earn). These include:

- Real estate (but not your primary home)
- Cash
- Bonds
- Stocks
- Savings
- Personal property (not including household goods and personal effects, like wedding rings)
- Vehicles (unless someone in your household uses them for transportation)

The SSA doesn't count your car, insurance policies worth less than $1,500, and burial plots you own as part of your resources. If your resources total $2,000 or less ($3,000 for a couple), you may be eligible for SSI.

HOW IS YOUR BENEFIT CALCULATED?

After the Social Security Administration has calculated your countable income, excluding the various things listed in the preceding pages, it subtracts this number from the benefit amount (currently $943 for individuals).

For example: John is sixty-three and suffers from diabetes, which makes him no longer able to work at his lifelong job. His Social Security benefit is $400 per month. This counts as income, but the SSA deducts the first $20 of it: $400 – $20 = $380. Now the SSA subtracts $380 from the current SSI benefit: $943 – $380 = $563. John is eligible to receive a monthly SSI benefit of $563. By applying for and receiving SSI benefits, he's more than doubled his monthly income.

Now let's look at a slightly more complicated example. Emily, sixty-four, is still working part-time but suffers from a disability. Her monthly wage is $317. She applies for SSI benefits. First, the SSA subtracts $20 from her wages since they count it as income: $317 – $20 = $297. Next, the agency subtracts the first $65 of her earned wages: $297 – $65 = $232. Finally, since $232 is more than $65, Emily's countable income is divided in half: $232 ÷ 2 = $116, so $232 – $116 = $116. The SSA now subtracts that from the current benefit amount for individuals: $943 – $116 = $827. This means Emily will receive an SSI monthly benefit of $827. That's in addition to any money she's receiving from Social Security, if she's already put in for benefits.

As a further qualification for SSI, you must live in the United States or the Northern Mariana Islands. You must also be a US citizen.

SSI Support for Mental Illness

Approximately 57% of SSI-only recipients have at least one mental health diagnosis. These include a wide range of issues from developmental disorders to autism to depression; these are conditions that can make it impossible for the person to work enough to support themselves over the long term. Many recipients of SSI due to mental illness are children and young adults, with most beneficiaries younger than retirement age.

HOW TO APPLY FOR SSI

The process for applying for SSI is the same as that for applying for disability benefits. The list of materials you should bring is similar. You will need:

- Birth certificate
- Social Security card (or other proof of your SSN)
- A mortgage if you own your own home; if you rent, a signed lease
- Information about your income, such as payroll slips, insurance policies, etc.
- Contact information for doctors, hospitals, and clinics where your disability has been treated
- Proof of citizenship
- Your checkbook or some other document that includes your bank account number

CHILDREN WITH DISABILITIES

Protecting Your Offspring

Approximately 1 million disabled children in the United States rely on SSI for financial relief. Families with disabled children often take on extraordinary expenses to care for their children, causing financial hardship. Autistic children, as well as those with Down syndrome or cystic fibrosis, for example, need additional support to survive and thrive. That may involve specialized equipment, home and classroom accommodations, or home health aides. Those costs can add up to thousands of dollars every year, not to mention lost work time for parents. In these situations, support from Social Security can be absolutely essential.

Many families aren't aware that this support exists. According to the SSA, applications to this program have been dropping steadily for nearly a decade. But advocacy groups are working to spread the word. The money is there to help families that qualify—an average of about $650 per month. Whether the child is under eighteen or now an adult, the SSA offers both monetary and other forms of support, like the Plan to Achieve Self-Support (PASS) program, which helps disabled children achieve career goals, or direct access to Medicaid (in many states). Though the application process can feel overwhelming at times, the benefits are worth fighting for.

IF YOU BECAME DISABLED IN CHILDHOOD

If you became disabled when you were younger than age twenty-two and are now an adult, you might be eligible for Social Security

Disability Insurance (SSDI). You can qualify for these benefits if either of these circumstances is true:

- At least one of your parents is receiving Social Security benefits; these can either be retirement or disability benefits
- At least one of your parents has died and had worked enough years to qualify for benefits

The key here is that as the "child," you don't need to have worked to receive the benefits. It's sufficient that one or both of your parents were qualified to receive them. Essentially, you piggyback onto your parents' benefits.

IF YOU'RE THE PARENT OF
A DISABLED CHILD

Your child may qualify for Supplemental Security Income if she or he is younger than eighteen (or under twenty-two and regularly attending school, in some cases) and has a disability that meets Social Security's definition. Additionally, your family's income and resources have to fall below the limits set by the Social Security Administration. This is because SSI is designed specifically for those who have low incomes and scarce resources.

Results May Vary

Even though the federal SSI benefit is the same, the amount your child receives may vary from state to state, since many states supplement SSI payments. For example, while a few states, including Arizona and Arkansas, don't offer state supplements to SSI, most states do tack on a state benefit.

The rules for income and resources are:

- Your child can't be working and earning more than $1,550 a month (for 2024)
- Whatever disability (or combination of conditions) your child has must severely limit his or her activities
- The disability must have been or be expected to last at least twelve months or result in death

Applying for Disability Benefits for Your Child

Just as you would if you were applying for disability benefits for yourself, you'll need to supply the SSA with very thorough information about your child's medical condition. They'll want permission from you to talk to your child's doctors, therapists, and teachers to determine the nature and extent of the disability. Be prepared to supply medical and school records. Just as with other kinds of disability benefits, this information is passed on to the Disability Determination Services office. The staff there will conduct the actual interviews with the people treating your child. It's possible they may ask your child to undergo an independent medical examination.

Immediate Payments

Even though, as with other benefits, it can take between three and five months to determine whether your child is eligible for disability benefits, SSI will begin payments immediately for certain conditions. These include:

- Symptomatic HIV
- Total blindness
- Total deafness
- Cerebral palsy
- Down syndrome
- Muscular dystrophy
- Severe intellectual disability (for children at least four years old)
- Low birth weight (below 2 pounds 10 ounces)

Even if the SSI ultimately decides against granting benefits, you don't have to pay this money back.

DISABILITY REVIEWS

Because some disabilities change over time, the Social Security Administration will regularly review your child's medical condition. If your child is expected to improve and is under eighteen, the review will occur at least once every three years. For low-birth-weight babies, the review will occur around their first birthday. At these reviews, you'll be expected to show that the disability continues to interfere with your child's ability to function normally.

When the child turns eighteen, the SSA conducts a further review, using adult disability rules.

IF YOUR CHILD WANTS TO WORK

As they grow into their teenage years, many children want to take a job to earn extra money or help support their families. SSA encourages this. For instance, the agency doesn't count most of your child's income when making the determination as to whether she or he is eligible for SSI benefits. If the child is below age twenty-two and attends school regularly, the SSA excludes $2,290 of their monthly income in their calculations.

Plan to Achieve Self-Support (PASS) Program

The Social Security Administration runs a program designed to help people with disabilities save money toward fulfilling a work goal. The program is called Plan to Achieve Self-Support (PASS). Once you determine what your work goal is (something you can do with the help of a vocational rehabilitation counselor), contact the SSA office and get a PASS form to fill out. A PASS counselor will work with you on achieving your goal. You must save the money from income other than your SSI benefits, but the SSA may increase SSI benefits once you enroll in PASS. The program is open to disabled children fifteen years or older.

MEDICARE

The government health programs Medicare and Medicaid will be discussed in more detail later on in this book. For now, suffice it to say that your disabled child can get immediate help from Medicare if she or he:

- Has end-stage renal disease and needs a kidney transplant or maintenance dialysis
- Has Lou Gehrig's disease (amyotrophic lateral sclerosis, or ALS)

Other Healthcare

The Social Security Act contains a provision for children with special healthcare needs. Under this provision, the SSA administers a series of healthcare programs. The SSI will refer you to them if your child is eligible for benefits. Even if she or he isn't eligible, the programs may be able to help you.

SPOUSAL BENEFITS

A Key Element of Social Security Claims

One of the most important features of the Social Security system is that it works for both you and your spouse. This can be the case even if your husband or wife never paid into the system.

To qualify for spousal benefits, you must be at least sixty-two and have been married to the principal breadwinner in the family for at least a year. There are some exceptions to this rule: If your spouse and you have been married to each other for less than a year but she or he is the biological parent of your child, the spouse qualifies for benefits. No matter what your age, you can receive spousal benefits if you're caring for your partner's child.

Finally, if you have been divorced from your spouse to whom you'd been married to for at least ten years, you may be eligible for Social Security benefits. This will be examined in greater detail later on in this book.

WHETHER TO FILE

Although your spouse may be eligible for spousal benefits, she shouldn't take them if her own benefit, which is based on her own work history, would be larger. Clearly, her (and your) objective should be to get the largest benefit possible. There are a variety of strategies to do this. Before diving into them, though, let's talk briefly about one strategy that no longer exists: file and suspend.

File and Suspend

Under previous Social Security rules, it was possible to file for benefits and then suspend them—that is, not take them—when you reached your FRA. Once you did this, your spouse could then apply *only* for spousal benefits (based on your work history). Meanwhile, your benefits would grow because you suspended them. Ideally, your spouse would take spousal benefits until you both reached age seventy, at which time both you and your spouse would take your own full benefits. Thus, rather than waiting to draw income from Social Security, one spouse would receive benefits while both of your benefits would grow.

This file and suspend strategy wasn't used by large numbers of people, mostly because they weren't aware of it. However, it began growing in popularity. At that point, the federal government decided to step in. In 2015, Congress passed a law that ended file and suspend as a viable option.

A similar, but not identical, strategy was also closed off in 2015. If you were born after January 1, 1954, you are no longer allowed to file what is called a restricted application—that is to apply only for spousal benefits. The object of this strategy was to file just for your spousal benefits. Because you delay taking your retirement benefits, your own benefits would grow. Then, when you reached age seventy, you would drop the spousal benefit and take your full benefit instead. It was a nice strategy, but sadly you're not allowed to use it anymore, unless your birthday comes before January 1, 1954.

When Is Ten Years Not Ten Years?

The Social Security rules get very pedantic when it comes to the ten-year rule about divorced spousal benefits. It's not just a total of ten years that you have to be married but ten *consecutive* years. For instance, if John and Mary were married from 2000 to 2010 and then divorced, Mary can collect spousal benefits based on John's earnings. But if they were married in 2000, divorced in 2006, remarried the following year, and divorced in 2015, Mary's out of luck. They were, in fact, married for a total of fourteen years, but the years weren't consecutive. From the SSA's viewpoint it doesn't count, so Mary will have to base her benefits on her own earnings record.

APPLYING FOR SPOUSAL BENEFITS

When applying for spousal benefits, you will need proof of your marriage and its date to establish that you've been married at least a year (a marriage certificate is fine). You'll also need proof of your age.

Same-Sex Marriage

As of June 2015, the date of the Supreme Court's ruling in *Obergefell v. Hodges*, same-sex marriage became legal in all states of the union. As a result, all married parties have the same rights in regard to spousal Social Security benefits. In fact, the SSA had granted such benefits to same-sex couples even before *Obergefell v. Hodges* in all states where same-sex marriage was legal.

In those states that recognize civil unions and domestic partnerships, the SSA will treat you as if you're married, and you can file for spousal benefits. Currently the states recognizing these relationships include:

- Connecticut
- Hawaii

- Nevada
- Oregon
- Vermont

Primary Insurance Amount (PIA)

It's time to reintroduce a term: primary insurance amount (PIA), which is the total amount of money a beneficiary is eligible to receive once she or he reaches full retirement age (FRA). This concept is important here because your spousal benefit can't exceed 50% of your partner's PIA. For instance, if Janet's PIA is $3,000 and her husband, Roger, decides to take spousal benefits, the highest such benefits can be is $1,500 (since $3,000 ÷ 2 = $1,500).

However, even though your maximum spousal benefit would be 50% of your partner's PIA, it can be less depending on the circumstances. For one thing, if you claim spousal benefits before reaching your FRA, the amount will be reduced for each month before your FRA (the exception to this is if the partner claiming the spousal benefits is taking care of your child and the child is under age sixteen).

The following table shows reductions in the 50% benefit depending how early you claim it.

AGE	PERCENTAGE OF PARTNER'S BENEFIT
65	45.8%
64	41.7%
63	37.5%
62	35.0%

As you can see, it pays to wait until reaching your FRA to claim spousal benefits—just as it does with your full retirement benefits. However, and this is an important difference, unlike your full retirement benefit, your spousal benefit does *not* increase if you wait to claim it until you're seventy years old. It can never go above that 50% of your partner's full benefit. On the other hand, if the partner taking full benefits waits until she or he turns seventy to claim, that 50% can be a significantly larger sum of money.

Use a Calculator

The Social Security Administration has a calculator to help give you a rough idea of what your spousal benefits would be. Go to www.ssa.gov/oact/quickcalc/spouse.html.

SURVIVORS BENEFITS

Living after the Breadwinner Is Gone

Few things are more devastating than the death of a family member, no matter whether it is unexpected or has been anticipated for some time. Apart from the emotional loss, there is often a significant financial impact, particularly if the deceased had been the family's primary breadwinner.

Social Security was designed as a way to help prevent families from slipping into poverty. Survivors benefits are an important way in which Social Security fulfills this function.

WHO'S ELIGIBLE?

Those in your family who may be eligible for survivors benefits include your widow or widower, children, and dependent parents. If you are divorced, your divorced spouse may be eligible as well.

For Social Security to pay these benefits, you must have worked at least ten years (except in certain circumstances, such as dying at a young age). In somewhat macabre fashion, the fewer the number of years you work beyond those ten, the greater the possible benefits paid to your survivors will be. The logic, of course, is that they had anticipated you working for many years more and are therefore more dependent on the money you would have earned.

Illness Before Dying

If you suffered from an illness before your death, it probably limited your ability to work. If, in the three years immediately preceding your death, you were only able to work one and a half years, the Social Security Administration will still pay benefits to your children and your widow or widower if she or he is looking after the children.

When to Take Survivors Benefits

As with retirement benefits, there are advantages to waiting before you take survivors benefits. A widow or widower can get full benefits by waiting until full retirement age to take them. Taking them early reduces the monthly amount. However, if she or he is taking care of a young child who is receiving Social Security benefits, there's no penalty for her or him to take benefits early.

If you have children under the age of eighteen, they can take benefits. Older children who were disabled before age twenty-two may also receive benefits. The Social Security Administration observes, "Under certain circumstances, we can also pay benefits to your stepchildren, grandchildren, step-grandchildren, or adopted children."

Remarriage

Many times people who've lost a spouse remarry. How does this affect their benefits? Essentially, it depends on how old you are when you remarry. If you're younger than sixty, your survivors benefits will stop. On the other hand, if you're older than sixty (fifty if you're disabled), you can continue to collect benefits based on your former spouse's earnings. After you turn sixty-two, you're eligible to collect spousal benefits based on your new spouse's earnings if that figure would be higher than what you were collecting before.

If your parents are financially dependent on you (that is, if you make up at least half of their financial support) and are at least sixty-two, they may be eligible for Social Security benefits if you precede them in death and that benefit exceeds their own. If you are divorced and your divorced spouse is at least sixty, she or he can get benefits provided the marriage lasted at least ten years. If she or he is caring for your child and that child is under sixteen or disabled, the widow or widower doesn't have to meet the ten-year rule.

Lump-Sum Death Payment

Social Security will make a one-time lump-sum death benefit payment of $255 to your survivor if one of these conditions holds:

- The survivor was living in the same household as you when the death occurred
- You and your survivor were living apart, but the survivor was receiving benefits on your employee record in the month you died
- The survivor became eligible for benefits upon your death

HOW MUCH?

Just as with normal retirement benefits, the more you made during your lifetime the better off your survivors will be. Your Social Security statement, accessible online through www.ssa.gov/myaccount, will tell you how much your survivors benefits will pay those you leave behind.

The SSA advises that if you're eligible for survivors benefits you should apply right away. This is because in some instances payments will be made from the time you apply and *not* from the time your spouse died. You can't apply for survivors benefits online. To report a death or apply for benefits, you can contact your local Social Security office or call 1-800-772-1213.

Documents you will need include:

- Proof of death (a death certificate or proof from a funeral home)
- Your Social Security number and that of the deceased
- Your birth certificate
- Your marriage certificate
- Your final divorce decree, if applicable
- Social Security numbers for any dependent children
- Your deceased spouse's W-2 forms or federal self-employment tax return for the most recent year
- Your bank account number and routing number (remember that Social Security payments are deposited directly into your account)

There is a limit on the amount of survivors benefits that can be paid to a family. Total family benefits are limited to between 150%–180% of the deceased's benefit amount.

The Social Security Administration gives these estimates of survivors benefits:

- A widow or widower, at full retirement age or older, generally gets 100% of the worker's basic benefit amount
- A widow or widower, age sixty or older, but under full retirement age, gets about 71%–99% of the worker's basic benefit amount
- A widow or widower, any age, with a child younger than age sixteen, gets 75% of the worker's benefit amount
- A child gets 75% of the worker's benefit amount

Pensions and Social Security

If your employer has a pension plan (something that's becoming pretty rare these days) and you've already paid Social Security taxes on it, receiving the pension won't have any impact on your Social Security benefits. On the other hand, if you get a pension from somewhere that's not covered by Social Security (for example, the federal government), the SSA may reduce the size of your benefit. (This will be discussed further in the section dealing with the Government Pension Offset.)

If you haven't reached your full retirement age, it's quite possible that you're still working. This income probably affects the size of the survivors benefit you receive. This will be discussed more in the section about working in retirement. For the moment, just know that there is an upper limit on earnings. If you exceed it while receiving benefits, the size of your benefit will go down. However, this will only affect *your* benefit, not those of other family members.

OTHER BENEFICIARIES

Who Else Can Get Benefits?

The Social Security Administration has to deal with a wide range of classes in administering benefits. These include veterans (both abled and disabled), American citizens living abroad, and qualified citizens of other countries. This section examines these participants in the Social Security system, and it explains any quirks or details in relation to their class.

VETERANS

Through the Veterans Administration (VA), if you are a veteran who has been wounded in the course of duty, you may be eligible for additional veteran benefits. Any number of conditions may cause you to be eligible, including (but not limited to) the following:

- Post-traumatic stress disorder (PTSD)
- Traumatic brain injury
- Post-concussive syndrome
- Military sexual trauma
- Exposure to toxic chemicals (including Agent Orange)
- Orthopedic injuries
- Injuries related to explosions
- Neurological injuries

Receiving veteran benefits does not automatically qualify you to receive Social Security disability benefits. The two sets of benefits have different standards. For instance, you can receive VA disability benefits for partial disability. However, the Social Security system requires that to receive disability benefits from the SSA you must be entirely unable to perform your job.

Expedited Benefits

If you became disabled while on active military duty, it's possible to expedite your Social Security benefits, assuming you're eligible for them. Go to www.ssa.gov/people/veterans for more information about how to do this.

MILITARY BENEFITS AND SOCIAL SECURITY

If you served in the US military after 1956, you qualify to receive both military benefits and Social Security benefits (if you served before 1957, you get partial Social Security credit for your service).

You can also be given, in some circumstances, extra credits for your military service. Remember that you need a total of forty credits to become eligible for Social Security benefits, so:

- If you served during the period from 1957 to 1967, the SSA adds extra credits to your earnings record when you apply for Social Security benefits. You are credited with $300 for each quarter in which you received active duty basic pay.
- If you served during the period from 1968 to 2001, the extra credits were automatically added to your record. For every $300

you earned in your military pay, you received another $100 in recorded earnings, up to a maximum of $1,200 per year.

- If you served after 2001, you don't receive any extra credits for your service.

GETTING SOCIAL SECURITY IF YOU'RE LIVING ABROAD

These days, in an effort to beat the cost of living (especially medical care), many American retirees are looking at moving to other countries. Many nations welcome these folks due to the money they spend, boosting national economies. But retirees often have questions about how living outside the United States will affect their Social Security benefits. The answer to this question depends on a variety of factors, such as if you're solely a US citizen or if you have dual citizenship.

What's Outside the United States?

Just to be clear, "outside the United States," means not living in any US territory, including Guam, American Samoa, Puerto Rico, the US Virgin Islands, or the Northern Mariana Islands.

If You're a US Citizen

If you're a citizen of the United States and eligible for Social Security benefits, the SSA will continue to pay those benefits into your bank account. However, this will not be the case if you live in one of the following countries:

- Cuba
- North Korea
- Azerbaijan

- Belarus
- Kazakhstan
- Kyrgyzstan

- Tajikistan
- Uzbekistan
- Turkmenistan

If you are living in one of these countries and travel to a country where the SSA can send your benefit payments, they'll generally do so. It's also possible in certain circumstances to receive your payment by going to the US embassy in the country you are staying. Your local Social Security office can explain these circumstances to you in more detail.

If You're a Citizen of Another Country

If you are an American citizen and become a citizen of another country and are still qualified for American Social Security benefits, you can continue to receive them, assuming you've already filed for them. If you are eligible and haven't yet started to claim them, you can still claim them, provided the country of which you're a citizen is one of the following:

- Austria
- Belgium
- Brazil
- Canada
- Chile
- Czech Republic
- Finland
- France
- Germany
- Greece

- Hungary
- Iceland
- Ireland
- Israel
- Italy
- Japan
- Luxembourg
- Netherlands
- Norway
- Poland

- Portugal
- Slovak Republic
- Slovenia
- South Korea
- Spain
- Sweden
- Switzerland
- United Kingdom
- Uruguay

REGULAR QUESTIONNAIRES

In order to cut down on fraud and keep track of its payments, the Social Security Administration sends out regular questionnaires to people who receive Social Security benefits abroad. If you don't return the questionnaire, your benefits will be stopped, which is a pretty good incentive to fill it out and put it in the mail.

Working in a Foreign Country

If you're working in a foreign country and are younger than your full retirement age, the SSA will not pay benefits for each month you work more than forty-five hours. It doesn't matter how many hours a day you work or how much you earn. The absolute limit is if you're working more than forty-five hours a month.

BENEFITS FOR CHILDREN

Protecting Young People

In the minds of most people, Social Security is associated with growing old and retiring. It's true that this is the way most people in the system experience it, but you've already seen that one part of Social Security is designed to help people with disabilities. Still another part aims to assist children.

More than 3 million children currently receive benefits from Social Security. For many of these, it's because their parent or parents are dead, disabled, or retired. Social Security payments help limit or prevent child poverty.

CHILDREN WHO ARE ELIGIBLE FOR BENEFITS

Of course, not all children can receive benefits. According to the SSA, one of the following two conditions must exist for a child to be eligible:

1. The child's parent must be disabled or retired and entitled to receive Social Security benefits
2. The child's parent must have died and have worked long enough to be able to start taking Social Security benefits

Additionally, the child must be unmarried, younger than eighteen (the child can also be eighteen or nineteen and a full-time student still in high school), or eighteen or older and disabled (provided the disability began before age twenty-two). So, while some children may qualify for benefits, it's not a common occurrence.

Children of Retired Parents

If your child is a dependent (under eighteen, attending elementary or high school, or has been disabled since before age twenty-two) and you're retired and taking Social Security benefits, your child is entitled to a benefit of up to 50% of yours. Because of the existence of the family maximum benefit rule, if you have several children who are dependents and can take benefits, each benefit will be smaller than if you only had a single child. Simply put, the more kids you have, the less each kid gets.

Spousal Benefits and Child-in-Care

If you married someone younger than you and you are sixty-two or older and have filed for benefits, your spouse can take benefits before reaching age sixty-two, provided that she or he is caring for a child (called a child-in-care by the SSA) who is either:

- Under the age of eighteen
- Mentally disabled and over the age of eighteen but who became disabled before age twenty-two

This can come in handy, especially if you need money right now to take care of your child, and it would be difficult to wait until you and your spouse both reached the claiming age of sixty-two.

Divorced and Child-in-Care

There's an exception to the rule about spousal benefits and child-in-care. If you're divorced and have a child-in-care, you can't get child-in-care spousal benefits on your living ex's record until you turn sixty-two.

Applying for Benefits

The kinds of documents you'll need to bring with your child when they apply for benefits depends on the circumstances. In any case you'll need the child's birth certificate and SSN, as well as the parent's SSN. If the parent is deceased, you'll need proof of that, either in the form of a death certificate or a note from a funeral home. If the child is disabled, you'll need medical records and contact information for the doctors, clinicians, therapists, and others involved in the child's treatment.

You should be prepared to provide the following information to the Social Security office:

- Your name and SSN
- The child's name, SSN, and relationship to you (or to the recipient of the Social Security benefits)
- If you're the child's legal or adoptive parent
- If you're the child's legal guardian
- Whether the child has lived with the recipient in the past eighteen months
- If you've ever been convicted of a felony
- Into whose bank account the child's benefits should be paid (be sure to bring your checkbook with your account and routing numbers)

Benefits end when the child turns eighteen. At that point, the SSA presumes that your child can start earning a living and accumulating her or his own credits toward Social Security.

Care of a Child

According to the SSA:

- If you're receiving benefits because you have a child in your care, the date your benefits stop can be different than the child's.
- If the child isn't disabled, your benefits will end when he or she turns sixteen.
- If the child is disabled, your benefits can continue if you exercise parental control and responsibility for a mentally disabled child. Your benefits can also continue if you perform personal services for a child who's physically disabled.

You may remember from an earlier section that there's a limit to how much Social Security will pay to any one family. The family maximum payment is generally 150%–180% of the qualifying parent's full benefit.

In Your Care

As of April 2024, approximately 3.8 million children receive Social Security benefits, totaling $3.4 million. More than half of those children are receiving survivors benefits and around a third are children of disabled workers.

TAXES ON SOCIAL SECURITY BENEFITS

Giving the Government What's Theirs

Wait a minute, some may say. We already paid taxes—the FICA payroll tax—just to get our Social Security benefit in the first place. Do you mean the federal government's going to tax us *again*? We thought we got past all that when we retired.

Well, yes and no. It's true that some portion of people receiving Social Security have to pay taxes on their benefits. This tax is supposed to be assessed on people at the upper end of the income scale—presumably people who can afford it—but in practical terms it affects more people than you'd expect.

Currently, about 40% of beneficiaries pay taxes on their benefits. Even if you count yourself among the lucky 60% who don't pay these taxes, you should still understand how taxes are figured on benefits so you don't have any nasty surprises come April 15th (the last day of the tax season).

FIGURING YOUR INCOME

The key to finding out if you owe taxes on your benefits is understanding how to calculate your "combined" income. This is different when you're on Social Security than when you had a full-time job.

To calculate your combined income:

1. Take half of your total Social Security benefits amount

2. Take your adjusted gross income, which includes all other taxable income, including wages, self-employment income, interest on savings, dividends, any money you earned from capital gains, and so forth
3. Take any nontaxable interest that you earned (such as from government bonds)
4. Add the three numbers together—this final tally is what the SSA regards as your combined income

If you file for benefits as a single person and your annual combined income falls below $25,000, you don't owe taxes on your benefits. If your combined income is more than $25,000 and less than $34,000, you will owe taxes on up to 50% of your benefits. If your combined income is above $34,000, you'll owe taxes on up to 85% of your benefits.

If you file as a married couple, the limits are higher: The lower limit is $32,000, and the upper limit is $44,000. (Please note that these numbers are as of January 2024; like most other Social Security benefits, they're subject to change by congressional action.)

EXAMPLES OF SOCIAL SECURITY BENEFITS TAX

How does all of this work in practice? More specifically, what taxes are actually taken out of your Social Security check?

Let's imagine you are a single person and have waited until your full retirement age of sixty-seven to claim your benefit. Your monthly benefit works out to $2,007. So, how do you know if you are going to have to pay taxes?

Case A

If you don't have any other income than Social Security, your combined income amounts to $12,042 ($2,007 × 12 months = $24,084 ÷ 2 = $12,042). This is below the limit of $25,000 for a single individual, so your benefits will be tax-free.

Case B

Now let's suppose that in addition to your benefits, you have several other sources of income. You take annual distributions from an IRA and your 401(k) account that add up to $16,000, and you do freelance work for your old employer, which generates an additional $5,000 per year. Now your combined income amounts to $33,042 ($12,042 + $16,000 + $5,000). Your combined income is more than $25,000 but less than $34,000, which is the upper limit for individuals. You'll owe taxes on up to 50% of your benefits.

Case C

What about filing as a married couple? Well, say that you and your husband have both reached your full retirement ages and claimed benefits. Yours is $2,007, and his is $1,836. To get your combined income, assuming you have no other sources of income, add the two benefits together, multiply by twelve, and divide by two. Your combined income is $23,058. You're below $32,000, which is the lower limit for married couples, so you're in luck. No tax is due on your benefits. However, if you were to have any other sources of income, you might exceed the limit, and so a portion of your benefits would be taxed.

YOUR TAX RATE

Note that the amount of money you pay in taxes on your benefits (assuming you're taxed on them) is determined by your marginal tax rate. The following table indicates what these rates are for 2024.

MARGINAL TAX RATE	SINGLE FILER INCOME	MARRIED, FILING JOINTLY INCOME
10%	Up to $11,600	Up to $23,200
12%	$11,601 to $47,150	$23,201 to $94,300
22%	$47,151 to $100,525	$94,301 to $201,050
24%	$100,526 to $191,950	$201,051 to $383,900
32%	$191,951 to $243,725	$393,901 to $487,450
35%	$243,726 to $609,350	$487,451 to $731,200
37%	more than $609,350	more than $731,200

If you must pay taxes on your benefits, you may find it advisable to use the services of a tax professional to determine precisely how much you owe. You may need to make estimated tax payments to account for this additional taxable income to avoid IRS penalties and interest for underpaid taxes. You may also want to do some tax planning to prevent being bumped into the next higher tax bracket if your income is close to the boundary. Working with a professional can help you navigate these potentially expensive issues.

WORKING IN RETIREMENT

The Pluses and Minuses of More Income

For many people, retirement means complete relaxation. A retired person can get up in the morning whenever they want, do things at their own pace, putter around the house and the yard, and generally relax. For some, this is the life they have been looking forward to all those years when they were working away at their job.

For others, though, retirement just means the freedom to work only when and because you want to, but not giving it up altogether. There's nothing wrong with either of these ways of viewing retirement; it's just a matter of which suits you better.

THE BENEFITS OF WORKING

There are excellent reasons to continue a full-time job until age seventy. Such a course may help increase the size of your benefit to its maximum amount, if you're earning more than in previous years. Conversely, there are compelling reasons to avoid taking your benefits before you reach your full retirement age. If you do this, you will permanently reduce the size of the benefit Social Security pays you each month. Naturally, for some people this isn't an option. There are all kinds of reasons why you might claim your benefits when you reach the age of sixty-two, the earliest point at which you can take them.

There are other significant benefits to continuing to work for as long as possible or until age seventy. They include:

- **Benefits packages.** Many employers offer benefits packages to their employees, which may include health insurance, life insurance, vision coverage, and other perks.
- **Savings plans.** Many companies offer their employees an opportunity to enroll in 401(k) plans or other employer-sponsored retirement plans, which are an excellent means of saving for retirement. In some, though not all, cases, employers will match a percentage of employee contributions to the plan, basically giving you free money.
- **A steady paycheck.** One of the biggest benefits of working, of course, is the prospect of a reliable weekly or biweekly check.

Of course, there are disadvantages of working late in life as well.

- **Despite government mandates against it, age discrimination exists in the workplace.** As you grow older, you may find it harder to get promotions or to move into different positions at work. You may watch as younger employees with less experience are promoted above you. And, of course, there is the danger of finding your position eliminated because your boss doesn't want to keep someone at your salary level on the payroll.
- **If you're let go, you'll probably find it harder to get a new job.** Most employers want to hire people who will stay with the company for a long time, not someone who they believe is going to retire in a few years.
- **Physically, continuing to work into your late sixties may be challenging.** Despite our best efforts to stay in shape, aging affects our bodies. People find it harder to perform some of the tasks at work that were easy to do when they were younger. Physical ailments may start to become a real problem: arthritis, and deteriorating vision and hearing, for example. And chances are it will be difficult (if not impossible) to maintain the energy levels you once had ten or fifteen years previously.

All of these are issues to consider when you're deciding when to stop working and start collecting your Social Security benefits. However, there may be an alternative to stopping work in order to collect Social Security benefits; let's talk about working *while* taking benefits.

ANNUAL EARNINGS LIMIT

The bad news is that Social Security places a limit on how much you can earn while taking benefits. The good news is that this limit ends once you reach your full retirement age.

How does the limit work?

As of 2024, the annual earnings limit if you're under your full retirement age is $22,320. For every $2 you earn above that limit, the SSA deducts $1 from your benefit.

For the year you reach your full retirement age, the limit goes up to $59,520 (this number is as of 2024 and is subject to change). In that year, the SSA deducts $1 for every $3 you earn above this limit.

Finally, when you pass your full retirement age, the limit goes away entirely, and your benefits are not affected by your earnings. Social Security then recalculates your benefit to give you credit for any years in which you didn't receive benefits because of your earnings.

Defining Earnings

When the SSA looks at your earnings, they count wages, bonuses, vacation pay, commissions, and self-employment income—basically any pay you receive for working. They do *not* count pensions, annuities, investment income, interest, or veteran benefits.

How Benefits Are Withheld

Generally, if your earnings put you over the limit, the SSA will hold back a certain number of months of benefits until the withholding amount that they calculated is met.

How does this work in practice?

Case A

Roger has turned sixty-two and qualifies for a monthly benefit of $1,500 if he begins his benefits now. If he waits until his full retirement age, which in his case is sixty-seven, his benefit will rise to $2,000. Roger's employer asks him to stay on as a part-time employee at an annual salary of $25,000.

If Roger takes his Social Security benefits now at age sixty-two, his total annual income will be $43,000 ($1,500 × 12 months = $18,000 + $25,000 = $43,000). That includes $25,000 of earnings. Since this $25,000 is above the $22,320 limit for earnings prior to full retirement age, some of Roger's benefits will be deducted – $1 for every $2 he's above the limit. This means Roger will lose $1,340 in benefits ($2,680 ÷ 2). He'll get a partial payment in the first month of $160 ($1,500 – $1,340), and then resume the $1,500 benefit.

Case B

Roger decides to keep working full-time for $65,000 and holds off on taking benefits for a while. It's now the year in which Roger will turn sixty-seven, his full retirement age. His birthday is in December, so that's when he'll actually reach FRA. The annual earnings limit has now risen to $59,520. Roger's salary of $65,000 is above the limit. He's over by $5,480 ($65,000 – $59,520 = $5,480). Since the SSA withholds $1 for every $3 he's over the limit, the total withheld from his benefits will be $1,826.67 ($5,480 ÷ 3). Since he hasn't yet reached full retirement age, his monthly benefits are now $1,900 per month. Therefore, the SSA will withhold from the first benefit check of the year, and he'll only get $73.33 that month before resuming to the normal payment of $1,900.

Thinking long term, it looks like it would have been better for Roger to not take benefits until he turned his full retirement age (in which case his benefit would have been $2,000 a month). However, there may be circumstances in which people feel compelled to start their benefits early.

TAKING BENEFITS EARLY

When It Makes Sense

As mentioned throughout this book, there are three times during which you can claim your benefits:

1. Between age sixty-two and your full retirement age
2. At your FRA
3. Between your FRA and age seventy

In this book, it has been suggested a number of times that it's generally better to *not* start your benefits early. This is because the size of your Social Security benefit will grow over time, if it's not taken. If you start collecting benefits at age sixty-two, you could be cheating yourself out of a substantial amount of money over your lifetime, but that's not always the most important factor. That said, an article in the news magazine *US News & World Report* commented that age sixty-two continues to be a popular age at which to take benefits, though its popularity has been declining:

> Age sixty-two is the earliest possible age you can sign up for Social Security retirement benefits. According to the SSA data, 22.9% of men chose this age to start to collect compared with 24.5% of women. The percentage of people signing up for Social Security at the minimum age has been declining over the years. For example, in 2014, 34.5% of men and 39.7% of women began receiving benefits at age sixty-two.

Deciding to take early benefits will depend on a number of factors, including general health and life expectancy, current financial situation, and the ability to continue working. While this guarantees a smaller benefit than waiting, it doesn't necessarily mean getting less total money over your lifetime. This is a highly personal decision based on specific life circumstances, and there are absolutely situations where taking early benefits makes the most sense.

A CASE HISTORY

For example, let's take Wilson, who was born in 1961. He's single, and based on his family history and his personal habits—he's a nonsmoker, a moderate drinker, and exercises during the week and on weekends—his life expectancy is somewhere around eighty-five.

Wilson has worked for most of his life, and when his boss mentioned switching him to part-time work, he jumped at the chance. He can't afford his current lifestyle on a part-time salary alone, so he considers taking his Social Security benefits. When he looks up his monthly benefit, he finds that it will be $1,883 monthly, or $22,596 annually. That combined with his part-time salary can help him cover all of his monthly expenses with enough left over to have some fun.

For a few years, this system works well. But when Wilson turns sixty-five, he loses his job. He has some retirement savings to draw from and, along with his Social Security benefits, he can make ends meet. He may need to find other ways to bring in a little money, maybe cut back on some expenses, and continue to enjoy his life. His retirement isn't as easy or carefree as he expected, but he's doing okay.

The Lower Benefits May Not Be Worth It

What would have happened if Wilson had waited five more years until reaching his full retirement age? His benefit would have been

$2,569 a month, or $30,828 a year, $8,232 more per year than his current benefit.

Assuming that Wilson lives to his estimated age of eighty-five, with his current benefits, he'll receive $519,708 over the rest of his life. This is a lot of money, but if he had waited until reaching his full retirement age, that sum would have become $554,904.

But there's a third alternative. Wilson could wait until he turns seventy to take his benefits. This will mean fewer years of retirement, of course, but the reward is his financial security.

If Wilson waits until he turns seventy to claim Social Security benefits, his monthly benefit will amount to $3,364 a month, or $40,368 a year. Assuming he lives to age eighty-five, he'll collect a total of $605,520. By waiting until age seventy, his lifetime payout from Social Security would increase by more than $85,000...but he would have had far less time to enjoy it.

Should You Make Investments?

One argument for taking early benefits is that you can invest all or a portion of the money and reap excellent returns. This assumes two things: First, you have another source of income that you can live on while your money is invested (at least until those investments start to pay dividends), and second, you know how to invest wisely.

Even if both are true, you can't predict market movements, and shorter-term investing tends to be riskier than longer-time horizons (five years or more) because there's less recovery time in case of a downturn. That said, careful investing can be a good way to outpace inflation and set up passive income streams for the future.

THE ISSUE OF LIFE EXPECTANCY

One very important factor in this decision is how long you're likely to live. The life expectancy table presented in the section Your Full Retirement Age can help you estimate this, but there are some other things you should take into consideration:

- **What's your family medical history?** If many of your family members have lived to a ripe old age in good health, there's a pretty good chance that genetics are going to work in your favor. If your parents or grandparents died young or had to deal with illness (like cancer or cardiovascular disease), that may be in your future. It pays to investigate your family history and try to get an average of the lifespans of the men and women who are part of it.
- **Do you smoke?** A 2018 study published in *Demography* reported smoking increases your risk of premature death from all causes, not just lung cancer and heart disease.
- **Do you drink?** Sure, most of us probably like to kick back with a beer or a glass of wine occasionally. But if you're a regular drinker (meaning you drink more than one alcoholic beverage every day), a 2022 study in *Nature* suggests you may be shortening your life expectancy by at least 6.9 years and increasing your risk of premature death from any cause by 43%.
- **Do you have a high-risk or high-stress job?** Some stress is inevitable with any job, but if you're feeling under constant stress, the hormones your body is producing will damage important tissue, knocking years off your life.
- **Do you eat a healthy diet and exercise regularly?** "Regularly" here means at least thirty minutes on most days. Walking or running counts, as well as any workout you do at the gym. A healthy

diet should include all the food groups, mainly whole plant foods, and avoid fatty, sugary, and processed foods.

Consider all these factors when you're deciding whether to take your Social Security benefits early. If you have any risk factors that affect your longevity, it might make sense to start taking your benefits as soon as possible.

WHEN DOES IT MAKE SENSE TO TAKE EARLY BENEFITS?

Even though the overwhelming majority of financial experts urge you to hold off taking benefits until you reach your full retirement age (and, if possible, until you reach age seventy), there are many reasons to start earlier.

Your Break-Even Age

One practical factor that can help you decide when to start taking Social Security Benefits is your break-even age—the age where it makes sense to have delayed taking benefits. Basically, how much you'll receive in cumulative benefits starting at age sixty-two, and when you'll surpass that by delaying. For example, let's say your benefit at FRA would be $3,000 per month, at sixty-two would be $2,100, and at seventy be $3,720. From age sixty-two to sixty-seven (most people's FRA), the total benefits received would be $126,000, and from sixty-two to seventy they would total $201,600. Your break-even age for waiting until age seventy would be 10.4 years, so you'd need to live until a little over age eighty to make that delay worthwhile. The math: $201,600 ÷ ($3,720 − $2,100) ÷ 12 = 10.4.

Do You Need the Money Now?

If you're struggling to work or having trouble paying all your survival expenses (such as housing, food, medicine, transportation, etc.), Social Security benefits can help reduce your financial stress. Many people reach the age at which they want to retire and rely on Social Security, even a reduced benefit, to pay the bills. This is particularly true for people who are finding it increasingly difficult to stay on the job or to find a new way to bring in money.

Is Your Life Expectancy Low?

If, after looking at charts and figures, you conclude that you're unlikely to live much beyond seventy or until your break-even age, it doesn't make much sense to wait until seventy to start taking your benefits. That's especially true if you want to have as long a retirement as possible, while you still have the most opportunity to enjoy it. In that case, claiming early benefits is probably the right thing to do.

Finally, it's worth pointing out that sixty-two is one of the more popular ages at which to claim benefits. So even though it usually makes more financial sense to wait, a lot of retirees want their money as soon as possible.

CLAIMING BENEFITS LATER

Increasing the Size of Your Benefit

It's a sad truth that many elderly people slip into poverty as they grow older. One of the most important reasons is rising medical costs and the need for increasingly expensive procedures designed to keep them alive. Another factor is that people underestimate how long they'll live, and they outlive their savings. This situation can be more difficult for people who took early Social Security benefits, thus permanently reducing the size of those benefits. They often discover that it is difficult to subsist on just the smaller sum from Social Security with no other streams of income.

The two best ways to avoid falling into this trap include increasing your savings by as much as possible, which will provide another source of retirement funds, and maximizing the size of your benefits as much as you can. To do either or both of these may involve some sacrifice now. The more you can save now, the more secure your financial future will be. Delaying Social Security benefits if you don't need them early will also add more financial security later with larger monthly payments.

TAKING THE CREDIT

The difference in taking your benefits at full retirement age and taking them at age seventy may be striking. For each year you work past your full retirement age, the government gives you a credit worth 8% of your benefits. In other words, if your retirement age is sixty-seven and you work three years past it to age seventy, your benefit grows by 24%.

BREAKING EVEN

One of the most common tools to determine whether or not you should take benefits early or wait it out is called a break-even analysis.

Expecting Beyond Expectancy

As said earlier, a lot of factors go into determining life expectancy. One of these factors has to do with how the life expectancy tables themselves are calculated. The basic calculation of life expectancy averages a cross-sample of males and females. This includes people who die when they're very young as well as very old. If you're a man, your expected lifespan is 73.5. But if you live to be sixty-two, your life expectancy increases to 81.3. For women who live to sixty-two, life expectancy increases from 79.3 to 84.04.

Essentially, a break-even analysis tells you how long you need to take benefits to receive the same monetary value you'd get if you took them earlier or later. Keep in mind the way benefits work: If you claim them before reaching your full retirement age, you get more checks, but they're smaller. If you claim at or after your full retirement age, there are fewer checks, but they're bigger. The break-even tells you at what age you'd have to reach under each scenario to get the same total amount.

Let's look at an example. Mark, who has just turned sixty-two, decides to claim his benefit of $750 per month. Linda, who is the same age, determines that she'll wait until her full retirement age of sixty-six, at which point her benefit will be $1,000. Neal, also turning sixty-two, decides to wait to claim until he turns seventy, when he'll claim $1,320 per month. The following table shows the cumulative amount of money they've received from Social Security.

BREAK-EVEN ANALYSIS FOR MARK, LINDA, AND NEAL (ANNUAL BENEFITS)			
Age	Mark	Linda	Neal
62	$9,000	$0	$0
63	$18,000	$0	$0
64	$27,000	$0	$0
65	$36,000	$0	$0
66	$45,000	$12,000	$0
67	$54,000	$24,000	$0
68	$63,000	$36,000	$0
69	$72,000	$48,000	$0
70	$81,000	$60,000	$15,840
71	$90,000	$72,000	$31,680
72	$99,000	$84,000	$47,520
73	$108,000	$96,000	$63,360
74	$117,000	$108,000	$79,200
75	$126,000	$120,000	$95,040
76	$135,000	$132,000	$110,880
77	**$144,000**	**$144,000**	$126,720
78	$153,000	$156,000	$142,560
79	$162,000	$168,000	$158,400
80	**$171,000**	$180,000	**$174,240**
81	$180,000	$192,000	$190,080
82	$189,000	**$204,000**	**$205,920**

Notice that even though Mark got money in years when Linda and Neal didn't, their totals caught up to his eventually and surpassed it. In Neal's case, this happened more quickly—by age eighty, after he'd been taking benefits for ten years. So, Neal's and Mark's break-even point is eighty, while Linda's and Mark's is seventy-seven. Neal's and Linda's is eighty-two. For Linda to break even by waiting, she'll have to live past age seventy-seven. Neal would have to live longer than age eighty to break even compared to Mark, and age eighty-two compared to Linda.

Keep in mind that this example doesn't include annual COLA increases. Both Linda's and Neal's payments would have increased by more than Mark's, which would affect their break-even ages.

"Social Security is based on a principle. It's based on the principle that you care about other people. You care whether the widow across town, a disabled widow, is going to be able to have food to eat."

—Noam Chomsky, American linguist

The Social Security Administration offers an online calculator that lets you see the difference in benefits when you start at different ages. You can find further information on early or late retirement by visiting their website: www.ssa.gov/OACT/quickcalc/early_late.html.

TAKING YOUR BENEFITS LATE

To circle back to the point made earlier: Unless there's a specific reason to do so, it may be better to not take your benefits earlier than your full retirement age. In fact, you'll get the biggest monthly payment if you can wait until age seventy before taking them. This means, assuming you live a long while, that you'll end up making more money in the long haul.

Consider the preceding example that compares Mark, Linda, and Neal. By the time they reach age eighty-five, Mark's total has reached $216,000, Linda's $240,000, and Neal's has totaled a whopping $253,440. That's more than $37,000 more than Mark. And that amount increases exponentially as the years advance. By age ninety, Mark's accumulated Social Security benefits amount to $261,000 but Neal by that time has benefits of $332,640. Now he's more than $71,600 ahead of Mark.

Social Security in Australia

The system of retirement benefits down under dates to 1992 and is called a Superannuation Guarantee. Unlike most social insurance systems, employees don't have to contribute to the fund, although they are encouraged to do so. Employers' contributions amount to 11% currently and will grow to 12% by 2025. Funds are divided into three types:

- **Preserved benefits.** These cannot be accessed by the employee until she or he turns fifty-five if born before July 1960, rising to sixty if born after June 1964.
- **Restricted non-preserved benefits.** These can be accessed under specific circumstances.
- **Unrestricted non-preserved benefits.** These can be accessed upon the worker's request, although certain conditions still apply.

All of this assumes—and this can't be stressed enough—that you've evaluated your probable life expectancy and all the factors that go into it. If there is a reasonable probability of you living well beyond your full retirement age, it might make sense to delay taking benefits if you can do so and enjoy the larger sums when they start.

IF YOU'RE SELF-EMPLOYED

The Challenge of Working for Yourself

As of 2023, approximately 15.8 million Americans were self-employed, about 10.1% of the working population. This is a significant number of people. For many, working for themselves is a lifelong dream—to be free of bosses, office routines, irritating coworkers...the list goes on. The thought of working out of your home and deciding your own hours and work goals is enormously attractive to many people.

However, Social Security can present concerns, and even shocks, to self-employed people. The fact is that although you work for yourself, you haven't opted out of US government-administered systems. And that means you will pay taxes.

SELF-EMPLOYMENT AND TAXES

In some ways, your tax situation as a self-employed person is far more complicated than if you worked for a company. For one thing, the company arranges for your taxes to be automatically deducted from your paycheck every fortnight (or however often you're paid). However, as your own boss you are now responsible for making sure that your taxes are paid—including the payroll taxes that fund Social Security and Medicare. If you earn more than $400 a year, you must file IRS Schedule SE (in addition to other forms).

If you work for an employer, matters regarding the Social Security tax are pretty simple. You pay 6.2%, and your employer pays 6.2% for Social Security; and both you and your employer pay the 1.45% tax to fund Medicare. However, if you're self-employed, the government assumes that you are *both* employer and employed. You have to pay both halves of the tax: 12.4% for Social Security and 2.9% for Medicare. That suddenly doubled tax burden can come as a shock—particularly in the early days of your self-employed career when your income isn't all that large and you're scrambling to find new gigs.

Deductions

The good news is that you're allowed to take some deductions you wouldn't be permitted to take if you worked for someone else. For example: When filling out Form 1040, you can deduct half your Social Security tax. However, this deduction isn't itemized; you take it from your gross income (the total of your income from all sources) when figuring your adjusted gross income (your gross income less certain special deductions, which include half of the self-employment taxes paid).

Wages and Self-Employment Earnings

If you have both wages paid by an employer and self-employment earnings, and if they total more than $168,600 (for 2024), you must pay taxes on the wages first. For example, if Roger earns $110,000 from his job and in addition makes $80,000 in freelance work from his self-employment business, his employer will withhold taxes on his wages. Roger will pay Social Security and Medicare on $58,600 on business earnings ($168,600 − $110,000 = $58,600) and will pay additional Medicare on the remaining $21,400 ($80,000 − $58,600 = $21,400) of business income because Medicare is not subject to a wage cap.

NET EARNINGS

For purposes of figuring your net earnings, Social Security counts your gross business earnings minus allowable business deductions, which include depreciation. When figuring your net earnings from your business, you should *only* include business income and expenses, but not your income from any other sources (like interest on your personal savings account, for example).

Common deductible business expenses include phone, Internet, software and apps, vehicle expenses, office supplies, insurance, payroll and payments to contractors, utilities, interest expenses (on business credit cards and loans, for example), depreciation (on business assets), accounting and tax prep fees, continuing education and training, and conferences.

Make sure to deduct all your business income and legitimate business expenses when figuring out your net income. You'll use the same net income number for both your income tax and self-employment tax calculations.

WHICH TAX FORMS TO FILL OUT

In any year in which your business earns $400 or more in net earnings, you need to fill out at least the following IRS forms:

- Form 1040
- Schedule C
- Schedule SE

Some taxpayers will need to complete additional forms, such as Form 8829 for home office expenses.

DEEMED FILING

Issues with Suspending Benefits

The economic world is constantly changing, and sometimes laws have a large impact on these changes. The passage of the Bipartisan Budget Act in 2015 had some significant effects on the way people could claim their Social Security benefits. One of these was in the area called "deemed filing."

The simplest explanation of deemed filing is that when you file for either your retirement benefits or your spousal benefits, you are "deemed" by the Social Security Administration to have filed for all the benefits to which you're entitled. In other words, the SSA treats an application for one set of benefits as an application for *both* retirement and spousal benefits, and it pays you the larger of the two.

WHAT CHANGED?

Prior to the Act's passing, the deemed rule only applied if you took benefits before your full retirement age. What Congress did through the Act was to extend this to full retirement age and beyond.

This rule change applies to you if you turned sixty-two *after* January 1, 2016. If you were sixty-two prior to this date, deeming only applies if you're taking benefits before reaching your full retirement age but not after.

It should be noted that this rule applies only to retirement benefits, not other kinds of benefits (disability, widow/widower, etc.). The exception is divorced spouses, where the new law does apply.

> "Deemed filing doesn't apply to widows and widowers. You can still file for only your own or only the widow(er)'s benefits, then switch to the other later. It's a great planning opportunity if you've lost a spouse or even an ex-spouse."
>
> —Andy Landis, author of *Social Security: The Inside Story*

An Example

Let's see how this works in practice. Janice and William are married. William has reached his full retirement age of sixty-seven, while Janice is only sixty-two. William files for his full benefits of $2,360 a month, and Janice files for her spousal benefits, which she calculates at $1,003, with the intent to take her own benefits later. When her first check arrives, though, she's startled to see that it's for a higher amount: $1,625. Puzzled, she contacts the SSA and is informed that the agency has deemed that even though she only filed for her spousal benefit, in fact she filed for both retirement and spousal benefits. Her regular retirement benefit is $1,625, which is obviously more than $1,003, and therefore the SSA is sending out her own retirement benefits and not spousal benefits.

This would be okay except that now Janice's benefit is permanently stuck at this pre–full retirement level (for age sixty-two). Even if she waits until age seventy, the amount of her benefit isn't going to go up.

Social Security in France

French Social Security is complicated. Some form of it has been in place since 1910. It is a voluntary system, ensuring retirement benefits for those who pay a tax of 6.65%. The employer pays 8.3%. To qualify, you must be at least sixty years old. There are also parallel schemes for survivors benefits, disability, and maternity.

With these relatively recent changes in Social Security, you must think long and hard before claiming benefits early. A mistake such as Janice's can cost you thousands and thousands of dollars in the long run.

"FILE AND SUSPEND" SUSPENSION

Another filing strategy that Congress eliminated was called "file and suspend." The strategy, the unintended result of several years of incremental changes to the Social Security system, had become increasingly popular as a loophole through which couples could maximize their benefits. Perhaps it shouldn't have come as a surprise that the government, looking to shore up the system, closed that loophole.

Here's how it worked. In 2000, changes to the law made it possible for workers to file for benefits and then suspend them. The suspended benefits would continue to gain delayed retirement credits (DRCs), meaning that when they were resumed, they'd be at a higher level. However, other benefits such as spouse and family benefits weren't suspended.

The practical upshot was that a worker could file and then immediately suspend his benefits, which would accumulate DRCs until he took them in the future. His spouse could file for spousal benefits and avoid taking her own benefit, leaving her benefits to grow until she reached her full retirement age (or seventy, if she could delay that long).

The Bipartisan Budget Act in 2015 changed this situation by mandating that after April 16, 2016, suspending one benefit has the effect of suspending *all* benefits. This change prevents the worker's wife or husband from claiming spousal benefits. The loophole, then, is effectively cut off.

The Bipartisan Budget Act also eliminated restricted application. A restricted application allowed a spouse to file for *only* spousal benefits. This scheme was essentially the answer to the deeming issue; without a restricted application, the person applying for spousal benefits would be deemed by the SSA to have applied for all her or his benefits and would have to take whichever benefit was larger: spousal or normal retirement benefits.

Phase-Out Time

Unlike the file and suspend strategy, which disappeared in April 2016, the restricted application rule didn't fully vanish until 2023. If you were born in 1953 or earlier, you could still have filed a restricted application, but all those eligible turned seventy in 2023. If you were born January 2, 1954, or later, the deeming rule applies to any applications you make for benefits.

WINDFALL ELIMINATION PROVISION

Working for Two Different Kinds of Employers

So far, this book has mostly discussed situations in which a person has worked their entire career in jobs under which they qualified for Social Security benefits. But of course, that's sometimes not the case. If a person worked for both an employer who withheld Social Security payroll taxes and one who didn't (for example, the federal government), their benefits may be affected by something called the Windfall Elimination Provision (WEP).

WHAT IS IT?

The WEP grew out of a simple fact about Social Security: The system, though it helps people from many different economic backgrounds, is designed to benefit lower-income people. To understand why this is the case, look at how the Social Security Administration calculates your benefits.

The SSA starts by figuring out your thirty-five top-earning years. As has been pointed out, if you only worked thirty years, the remaining five years will be counted as zeros (no income). Then the SSA adds up all your earnings for your top-earning thirty-five years, any zeros included.

That total earnings number is divided by 420 months (which is thirty-five years). This gives your average monthly earning during those thirty-five years (also known as average indexed monthly earnings or AIME).

Now the SSA does some calculations with the AIME using dollar amounts called "bend points" that change periodically. They multiply the first $1,174 by 90%. Then, they multiply the amount from $1,174 through $7,078 by 32%. Finally, whatever is left above $7,078 they multiply by 15%. The SSA adds these three sums together, and the result is your monthly benefit if you retire at your full retirement age.

An Example

Let's see how this works. Take a look at Ron, whose full retirement age is sixty-seven. SSA looks at his highest-earning thirty-five years. Because of bouts of unemployment and schooling, Ron didn't work for seven of those years, so for SSA purposes they count as zero earnings. Nonetheless, the total of these years is a whopping $3,264,874.

Now the SSA divides this number by 420. This means Ron's AIME is $7,773.51. Round it down to the nearest dollar, just as the SSA does. The first $1,174 of this is multiplied by 90%, giving us $1,057 (rounded to the nearest dollar). Then, they take $5,904 (the amount of AIME between $7,078 and $1,174) and multiply it by 32%. That gives us $1,889. Finally, they take $695 (the amount between $7,773 and $7,078) and multiply it by 15%, which gives us $104. Add those three numbers together, and you get $3,050. Thus, Ron's monthly benefit will be $3,050 if he retires and starts taking his benefits at his full retirement age.

For comparison purposes, let's look at Marcie, whose full retirement age is also sixty-seven. Her AIME is less than Ron's; it's $4,224. Ninety percent of the first $1,174 of this is $1,057. Then, the SSA takes $3,050 (the amount of Marcie's AIME remaining) and multiplies it by 32%, giving us $976. The SSA adds the $1,057 to the $976 and determines Marcie's monthly benefit to be $2,033 when she reaches her FRA.

SOCIAL SECURITY BENEFITS LOW-INCOME WORKERS

As the Center on Budget and Policy Priorities remarks, Social Security benefits are progressive: they represent a higher proportion of a worker's previous earnings for workers at lower earnings levels. For example, benefits for someone who earned about 45% of the average wage and then retired at age sixty-five in 2023 replaced about half of his or her prior earnings. But benefits for a person who always earned the maximum taxable amount replace only about 30% of his or her prior earnings, though they are larger in dollar terms than those for the lower-wage worker.

Consider our examples of Ron and Marcie. Ron's monthly benefit of $3,050 is higher than Marcie's benefit of $2,033. However, his benefit only replaces 39% of his average monthly earnings when he was working. Marcie, on the other hand, replaces 48% of her average monthly earnings.

Cost-of-Living Adjustment

Unlike your 401(k) or pension (if you're lucky enough to have these things), Social Security benefits are adjusted for inflation. This can be especially important in times of economic turmoil, when too often your investments are at the mercy of the markets. During the Great Recession of 2008, many couples lost much or all their retirement savings when the stock market crashed. But Social Security benefit payments were unaffected by the downturn.

Why the Windfall Elimination Provision?

Up until 1983, if your primary job wasn't covered by Social Security (for example, if you worked for the federal government), but then you switched to a job that *was* covered by Social Security, you'd be treated by the SSA as if you were simply another long-term low-wage worker. You had a lot of zeros on your earnings record, so your AIME would be low. But oddly, this gave you an advantage. You received a higher percentage of your Social Security–covered income compared to someone who had a higher primary insurance amount (PIA), plus you received a pension from your primary job.

The way the WEP works is that the 90% element of the SSA's formula is reduced and phased in for workers who reach sixty-two or became disabled after 1985. In some instances, the 90% can be reduced to as little as 40%.

The effect of this is to level the playing field a bit. The formula the SSA uses is based on the number of taxed years you worked (that is, the number of years you were taxed for Social Security—this is referred to as "substantial earnings").

NUMBER OF YEARS OF SUBSTANTIAL EARNINGS	PERCENTAGE USED IN SSA FORMULA
30+	90%
29	85%
28	80%
27	75%
26	70%
25	65%
24	60%
23	55%

22	50%
21	45%
20 or fewer	40%

However—and this is an important qualification of this rule—your benefit under the WEP generally won't be reduced to less than half the size of the pension you receive from the time you worked for a non–Social Security taxing company.

WEP Affects Millions

Nearly 3% of all Social Security beneficiaries—around 2.1 million people—were affected by the WEP as of December 2023. The vast majority of those people were state or local government employees. There are proposals in the works to change the way this law works to a more proportional formula from both types of employment to help increase the program's fairness.

As well, the WEP doesn't apply to you if:

- You're a federal worker and were first hired after December 31, 1983.
- You were employed on December 31, 1983, by a nonprofit that at first didn't withhold Social Security payroll taxes but later did.
- Your only pension is for work as a railroad employee.
- Your only work on which you didn't pay payroll taxes for Social Security was before 1957.
- You have thirty or more years of substantial earnings covered by Social Security.

GOVERNMENT PENSION OFFSET

If You Used to Work for the Government

Pensions, although increasingly disappearing from private companies, are still very much around in federal, state, and local government jobs. It's possible, given the financial crisis that seems to be gripping most states and big cities, that in time many of these may also vanish. But for right now the Social Security Administration needs rules in place to deal with them. This book has already shown one such rule: the Windfall Elimination Provision. Now it's time to look at another: the Government Pension Offset.

WHO IT AFFECTS

This provision is aimed at people taking spousal benefits and benefits for widows and widowers. If you're in this category and have a pension from the government (federal, state, or local; doesn't make a difference), the SSA will reduce your benefits by two-thirds of your pension.

"Social Security is not a retirement savings plan; it is a social insurance program. It's a contract that says, as a society, we will look out for you and your family when you can no longer work."

—Jeff Bingaman, former US senator

Consider Martha. Her husband, Randall, died, leaving her a widow at age sixty-four. Her survivors benefit ought to be $900 a month. But Martha, when she was younger, worked for the US Postal Service. Her pension payment from the postal service comes to $600. Two-thirds of that is $400, so the SSA reduces her monthly survivors benefit to $500 a month ($900 − $400 = $500). Even if Martha chooses to take her postal service pension in a single lump sum, it won't make a difference; the SSA will calculate what her monthly payments would have been and reduce her survivors payments accordingly.

When Benefits Are Offset

When Social Security first started, it was common for a man to be the breadwinner of the family and for a woman to stay home. Now, for many reasons, that's no longer the case. In order to hold the line of its costs, the Social Security system offsets survivors or spousal benefits if they're lower than the spouse or survivor's own benefits. For instance, as the SSA explains in a paper (available on their website), "If a woman worked and earned her own $800 monthly Social Security benefit but was also due a $500 spouse's benefit on her husband's record, we couldn't pay that spouse's benefit because her own benefit offsets it."

Exceptions to the Government Pension Offset Rule

There are some circumstances in which even if you have a government pension your spousal or survivors benefits won't be reduced. These include:

- If you get a government pension that's not based on your earnings.
- If, in addition to getting your pension, you paid Social Security taxes on your government job. This includes the further conditions that:

- You filed for and were entitled to spousal or survivors benefits before April 1, 2004, or
- The last day you had the job from which you're entitled to a pension was before July 1, 2004, or
- You paid Social Security taxes during the last sixty days you worked for the government.
- You switched from the Civil Service Retirement System (CSRS) to the Federal Employees Retirement System (FERS) after December 31, 1987. In addition:
  - You have to have filed for and be entitled to your spousal or survivors benefits before April 1, 2004, or
  - Your last day of working for the government was before July 1, 2004, or
  - You paid payroll taxes to Social Security for sixty months or more sometime after January 1988.
- You received (or were eligible to receive) your government pension before December 1982 and were also eligible for spousal benefits under the rules prevailing on January 1977.
- You received a government pension before July 1, 1983, and were already receiving one-half support from your spouse.

Whew! That's a lot of rules to take in. The basic point to come away with from all this is that if you get a government pension, it's going to affect your benefits. Overall, you'll still get money from the government, but you won't get your full Social Security benefits. You can see how much by using the Government Pension Offset calculator on the Social Security website at www.ssa.gov/prepare/government-and-foreign-pensions.

THE RETROACTIVE LUMP-SUM OPTION

Getting a Chunk of Money All at Once

Applying for your benefits as soon as you reach your FRA is a sound strategy for maximizing the amount of your monthly check (assuming you don't want to wait until you turn seventy). However, you may want to wait a bit longer past FRA before you apply for benefits. Specifically, you may want to take advantage of a little-known option called the retroactive lump sum. This option allows you to receive several months of retroactive benefits in one lump sum—that is, you get a bunch of cash right up front. Here's how it works.

GETTING A CHUNK OF CHANGE

Let's imagine that in 2024 Anne reaches her FRA of sixty-seven. She's entitled to a monthly benefit of $1,758. However, rather than immediately applying for benefits, Anne elects to wait a year. By doing this, she may qualify for a retroactive lump-sum payment of up to six months' worth of benefits—$10,548.

Downsides
This option can make sense if you've received some bad health news and don't believe you'll live very long but want to pay down some debt immediately. It can also make sense if you want to take that money and invest it. However, be aware that many—in fact, most—people who take this benefit with investing in mind don't, in

fact, invest the money. Rather, they spend it on various immediate necessities, and before they know it, the money's gone.

"You can look at history of these things, and Social Security wasn't devised to be a system that supported you for a thirty-year retirement after a twenty-five-year career… So there will be things that, you know, the retirement age must be changed, maybe some of the benefits have to be affected, maybe some of the inflation adjustments have to be revised."

—Lloyd Blankfein, American business executive

There is another downside that is not readily apparent. When you take a retroactive lump sum, the SSA fixes your regular monthly benefit back to the date where the lump-sum payout began accruing. In Anne's case, she took a six-month lump-sum payout when she was at FRA plus one year. In other words, for Anne, her monthly benefit will now be calculated as if she had started taking it at age sixty-seven and a half (not sixty-eight). Another significant consideration is that the retroactive lump-sum payment boosts your provisional income for the year, potentially taking you into a higher tax bracket such that some significant portion of your benefits will be taxed.

Who Can Claim This?

Despite the downsides, receiving a lump sum totaling six months' worth of benefits understandably has a lot of appeal. Unfortunately, Social Security has a complicated set of provisions for who can take what amount, and when:

- If you were born on or before April 30, 1950, you can claim the retroactive lump-sum benefit and, significantly, you can make it retroactive to any point after you reached your full retirement age.
- If you were born after April 30, 1950, you can still take the lump-sum benefit, but you can only make it retroactive to six months before you file.

It's worth noting that if you reached full retirement age on or before April 30, 2016, and have filed and suspended your benefits (you may remember from earlier that the file and suspend strategy is no longer allowed under new Social Security rules), you have much greater flexibility in taking the lump-sum benefit, with the understanding that doing so will freeze your benefit amount at whatever point you take the retroactive payment. Following is an example of how this might work in the real world.

Social Security in Germany

Germany, in some respects, is the home of Social Security systems, since the original idea of social insurance began with Chancellor Otto von Bismarck. To qualify, you must be at least sixty-five years old with at least five years of contributions to the system. If you're disabled, you may qualify to receive benefits at age sixty-three. There are also provisions for survivors' coverage, orphans, and permanent disability. These are all funded by joint contributions of employee and employer.

Barry was born on January 1, 1948. His primary insurance amount (PIA)—the amount of his benefit upon reaching his full retirement age of sixty-six—will be $2,024. In 2014, at age sixty-six, he filed for benefits and then suspended them. Then, two years later in 2016, he filed for a retroactive lump-sum benefit and requested that it be considered retroactive to the point he reached his full retirement age. His lump-sum payment will be $48,576 ($2,024 × 24 months). However, his monthly benefit, which he now starts receiving, will be $2,024. If he hadn't taken the retroactive lump-sum benefit and instead had simply started his benefits in 2016, his monthly benefit would have been $2,361 since his PIA increases by 8% each year he doesn't take benefits.

Still, even though his monthly benefits aren't as high as they'd have been if he'd delayed taking them, Barry made the right choice. His lump-sum payment helped pay down his mortgage, making it easier for him to meet his monthly budget.

STOPPING YOUR BENEFITS

The Strategy of Waiting

Let's consider Norman. He's sixty-two and has been working at the same company for most of his life. Now, with his wife retired and his children moved away and with children of their own, he's ready to close his cubicle and retire. He knows he's retiring before his FRA, but his monthly benefit of $1,845 seems like it will serve its purpose. In addition, his wife's Social Security benefits and careful withdrawals from their savings should enable them to live a reasonably comfortable lifestyle. He announces his retirement to his boss and applies for benefits.

Six months go by. Norman is happy, although he wishes sometimes that money wasn't so tight. Then, he gets a call from his old boss. It seems the company has taken on a new project. It's expected to take about five years to complete, and the boss wants to know if Norman would come back and work on it at his old salary. Norman wonders what he should do.

STOPPING BENEFITS BEFORE YOUR FRA

Norman knows that if he continues to take benefits while going back to work, he'll exceed his provisional income limits to the point that his benefits will, effectively, disappear. However, the job offer is too good to turn down. Luckily, since Norman took his benefits before his FRA, and because it's been less than a year since he filed, he has the option of stopping his benefits. The downside is that Norman is going to have to repay the SSA the six months' worth of benefits he's already received—that is, $11,070. Moreover, Norman's repayment must include any other benefits received by his family that were the result of his filing (spousal benefits, children's benefits, etc.). The SSA makes sure that there are no surprises to these family members: Anyone who received such benefits and is now repaying them must sign a form consenting to Norman's withdrawal of his request for benefits.

How Are We Compared to the World?

As of January 2024, the average Social Security benefit amounted to about $22,800 a year ($1,907 per month). How does that compare to other programs around the world? The answer is, not very well. Out of forty-seven countries, the United States ranked twenty-second in benefits. The top five nations are:

- Netherlands
- Iceland
- Denmark
- Israel
- Australia

  The lowest nation on this list is Argentina.

All of this certainly presents Norman and his wife with some challenges. But the upside is that now he can wait until he reaches his FRA to start claiming benefits again, at which point his benefit will have grown 8% per year to a nice $2,508 per month. He'll be getting almost $8,000 per year more in benefits when he retires at his FRA of sixty-seven.

AT FULL RETIREMENT AGE

Suppose Norman had retired at sixty-three but didn't receive the offer from his old boss until he'd passed his sixty-seventh birthday. In this case, Norman could have requested a voluntary suspension of benefits. He could do this up to the age of seventy, after which he'd have to continue to take benefits and couldn't stop them.

"The economist John Maynard Keynes said that in the long run, we are all dead. If he were around today, he might say that, in the long run, we are all on Social Security and Medicare."

—Ben Bernanke, American economist
and former chairman of the Federal Reserve

The great advantage of taking a voluntary suspension when you've suddenly got a new source of income is that you start accumulating DRCs (delayed retirement credits) that lead to an increase in your benefit. There are some significant advantages in doing this, since later in your life is when you're likely to need a higher benefit to cope with medical expenses. However—and this is very important—under the rules for Social Security passed in 2015, once you suspend your retirement benefits you are deemed by the SSA to have suspended *all* benefits, including spousal, family, and anything else you've claimed. Furthermore, if you voluntarily suspend your benefits, any benefits you receive that are based on someone else's earnings record will be suspended. You should certainly take this into consideration when debating whether or not to stop your benefits.

APPEALING AN SSA DECISION

Getting the System to Change Its Mind

With such a complex system involving so many people, it's inevitable that many of the SSA's decisions are going to be unpopular with applicants. This section examines how you can appeal an SSA decision.

DISABILITY BENEFITS

Probably the biggest area for disagreement between the SSA and the general population is with disability benefits. This is especially true because, if you remember, the SSA looks not just at whether your disability prevents you from doing your old job but whether it also prevents you from doing any related jobs that require similar experience and/or training. It's possible that the SSA has denied you disability benefits on the grounds that even though you can't do your old job, there are still several related jobs they believe you can perform. You, on the other hand, with a more intimate knowledge of what's actually involved in the job, disagree.

You can file your appeal online at https://secure.ssa.gov/iApplsRe/start. Doing so will speed up the process of the appeal, ensuring a timelier decision from the SSA. If the SSA denies your benefits, they will notify you by letter. They assume their letter takes five days to be delivered, and you have sixty days from receipt of that letter to file an appeal.

Levels of Appeal

There are four levels of appeal:

1. Reconsideration
2. Hearing before an administrative law judge
3. Review by the Appeals Council
4. Hearing in a federal court

Reconsideration

In this stage, someone who wasn't involved in the original consideration of your claim goes over your application and the reason it was denied. You have the opportunity at this step to provide additional information to bolster your claim. Although few claims are reinstated at this stage, it's important to make sure that your claim wasn't denied because of a simple administrative glitch. As with your initial appeal, if the reconsideration stage denies your claim, you have sixty days from the receipt of the SSA's letter to file an appeal to the next stage.

Timely Appeal

If you miss the sixty-day window to file an appeal, that may be used by the SSA as a basis for denial of your claim. There are some exceptions to this, but they're few and far between. In short, if you miss your appeal deadline, you'd better have a good reason that you can back up with proof. Otherwise, your appeals process will be stopped dead in its tracks.

Hearing Before an Administrative Law Judge

The date of the hearing will be set by the judge's office based on her or his schedule. It may be anywhere from several months to a year from the filing of the claim. The judge's office will send you a letter at least seventy-five days before the hearing, letting you know its time and place. You can waive this seventy-five-day period if you want your hearing expedited, but that does not guarantee it will be. Plus, the hearing will usually be within seventy-five miles of where you live. If you will have trouble traveling to the meeting, notify the SSA. If the reason is medical, send along a doctor's report confirming it. It's possible in many instances to hold the hearing by video so you can remain in the comfort of your own home. If the hearing is, for some reason, more than seventy-five miles from your home, the SSA may pay your transportation costs and even, subject to the approval of the judge, such expenses as meals and lodgings. To get coverage for these costs, you'll need to submit a written report to the judge at the hearing or as soon as possible afterward.

Given that this is a formal hearing, most experts strongly recommend that you be accompanied by a lawyer and that you bring all your documentation of your disability with you. This documentation can include such things as:

- Medical records
- Affidavits from doctors and/or therapists
- Prescription receipts
- Records of hospital stays

Whenever possible, bring the originals of these documents. Additionally, bring any extra evidence you'd like the judge to consider in making her decision.

Faxing the Evidence

According to the SSA, if your case is electronic, evidence can be faxed into the claim file using a special fax number and barcode provided by the hearing office or sent by your representative through Electronic Records Express (ERE) at www.ssa.gov/ere.

Since the SSA is highly experienced in its own rules and regulations, to say nothing of handling thousands of appeals such as yours, its representatives at the hearing will be experienced and knowledgeable. Look for a lawyer who is experienced in Social Security appeals. Remember, this is an important financial issue for you, and you won't help yourself by being cheap in the matter of legal representation.

When the judge asks you questions about your case, you will be under oath, and your testimony, as well as the rest of the proceedings, will be recorded. After the hearing, the judge will issue a written opinion upholding or denying your claim.

Tell the SSA about Your Lawyer

If you're going to bring a lawyer with you to the hearing, the SSA wants to know about it. Fill out form SSA-1696 Claimant's Appointment of a Representative and send it in before the hearing.

Review by the Appeals Council

The Social Security Appeals Council is the next step if you disagree with the administrative law judge's decision. It is in and around the Washington, DC, area, and filing an appeal before this court may involve traveling there. As with the administrative hearing, it's important to submit any new evidence and to make your case clearly and succinctly in writing (your lawyer can help you with this). You have sixty days after the original decision was handed down to file your appeal.

The council will consider your case and decide if the administrative hearing made a mistake in rejecting your claim. If they choose that course of action, they can either decide the matter for themselves or send it back to the administrative judge for further consideration.

Hearing in a Federal Court

Your court of last appeal, so to speak, is the federal court. This can be an extremely expensive process, and you shouldn't undertake it lightly. But if you feel that everyone in the appeals process thus far has misjudged your case, you have this option open to you. You have sixty days after receiving the Appeals Council's decision, including the decision to not review your case, to file this civil action.

BE AWARE OF THE ODDS

Appealing a claim, whether it is for a disability or something else in the Social Security system, can be a frustrating and an emotionally draining business. There's potentially a lot of money at stake for you and your family, so it can be worth it to try. In many respects, we're talking about your whole future. That's why it's important to go into this process with realistic expectations. Only about 10% of cases win during the reconsideration process, and around 35% win overall during the more formal appeals process. On top of that, there's a big backlog of around a million cases, so be prepared to wait. To give your claim the best chance of success, be calm, detailed, and thorough throughout the process. Take what time you need to gather the evidence for your appeals process. It's far better to have too much evidence than too little.

HEALTH AND SOCIAL SECURITY

Healthcare in Your Golden Years

Healthcare and Social Security may seem like two different topics, but they're intimately connected to one another. Healthcare is probably the single biggest expense you'll have as you grow older. Medical science keeps finding ways to keep people living longer. That's nice, but that also means every person has to find ways of stretching out their savings and ensuring they have access to medical care. This book has stressed that the issue of life expectancy is among the most important factors in considering your Social Security benefits and how they fit in with the rest of your retirement savings plan.

WHERE DOES HEALTHCARE STAND IN THE UNITED STATES?

Sadly, even after many years of debate and discussion and trying various ways of providing healthcare to its population, the United States ranks dead last among wealthy nations when it comes to a number of healthcare metrics (including quality, access, efficiency, equity, and healthy lives). The US population spends the most (by far) on healthcare but has a greater chance of developing multiple chronic health conditions and has shorter life expectancy. This assessment is not hearsay but comes from a 2023 study by the Commonwealth Fund, a private foundation dedicated to supporting research on healthcare issues.

Healthcare issues will continue to be a political football for some time to come. One thing most people *seem* to agree on, though, is that they want Medicare expanded, or at least left alone.

MEDICARE: WHERE'D IT COME FROM?

Medicare is much more recent than most of the Social Security system. It started out as a way for the government to provide medical care to the families of those serving in the armed forces. This was accomplished through the Dependents' Medical Care Act of 1956. Then, in 1965, President Lyndon Johnson signed Medicare into law as part of Title XVIII of the Social Security Act. The program's stated intention was to offer medical care to people sixty-five and older.

Medicare and Civil Rights

Medicare played a role in the 1960s burgeoning civil rights struggle by declaring it would only pay health providers if they integrated their facilities.

The program is administered through the Centers for Medicare and Medicaid Services, but the SSA is intimately involved too. Indeed, a great deal of information about Medicare is available on the SSA's website, www.ssa.gov. Basically, the SSA determines if you're eligible for Medicare and decides if you're entitled to Low-Income Subsidy (also called the Extra Help program—more on that later).

The Medicare program has expanded a number of times over the years, the most recent being coverage of most prescription drugs in 2003 under President George W. Bush.

WHAT DOES IT DO?

Medicare offers health insurance to those sixty-five and older. It also provides coverage for people with disabilities, kidney failure, and ALS, better known as Lou Gehrig's disease. It covers more than 48 million people, although it doesn't cover all medical expenses. Nonetheless, for millions of people it's their primary means of medical insurance.

It's divided into four parts, which are called, somewhat unimaginatively, Part A, Part B, Part C, and Part D. These are usually characterized as follows:

- Part A is called Hospital Insurance.
- Part B is called Medical Insurance.
- Part C is called Medicare Advantage, or fee-for-service.
- Part D is called prescription drug coverage.

This book will cover all these different parts in more detail in the next section. Each has its own defined roles within Medicare.

MEDICAID

Along with Medicare, the other prong of Social Security–related government healthcare is Medicaid. This program is designed to offer healthcare benefits to low-income families. It significantly expanded under the Affordable Care Act (known colloquially as "Obamacare") in many states, but some have made cutbacks since. For example, Wyoming, Kansas, and Georgia have not participated in Medicaid expansion.

Medicaid is a product of President Lyndon Johnson's Great Society—the series of social reforms he launched in his first full term. In 1965, Congress added Title XIX to the Social Security Act, under which states were to receive matching funds from the federal government to provide medical care to families unable to pay for it themselves. Thus, Medicaid is funded at both the federal and state levels.

And although it's a federal program, Medicaid is largely administered at the state level. Currently, Medicaid provides care for more than 90 million people. Unlike Social Security, Medicaid isn't just for people of a certain age; its beneficiaries include children and young people.

Medicaid is a means-tested system, as you'd expect of a program designed to help those with low incomes. States decide on their own eligibility criteria but must keep them within federal guidelines. Generally, the system considers income in relationship to the federal poverty level, which, as of 2024, is $31,200 for a family of four (this figure is updated every year to take inflation into account).

This book will further address Medicaid later. For now, it's important to understand how you qualify for Medicare.

Medigap

Because Medicare does not cover all medical procedures, many people purchase additional insurance plans to deal with the gaps in coverage. These plans are known as Medigap, and they vary by state. Depending on the policy, Medigap plans may cover things like Medicare copayments and deductibles and foreign travel emergency care.

WHO'S ELIGIBLE FOR MEDICARE?

The most basic thing you must do to qualify for Medicare is live until you're sixty-five. You must also be a US citizen or have been a legal resident for at least five years. You or your spouse must have paid Medicare taxes for at least ten years.

You can get Medicare benefits if you're younger than sixty-five, provided that you're disabled and have been receiving SSDI benefits or disability benefits through the Railroad Retirement Program for at least twenty-four months. You can also qualify if you have end-stage renal disease or need a kidney transplant.

Who Pays?

Medicare is paid for through payroll taxes in the same way as Social Security. Plus, monthly premiums are deducted from Social Security checks. Currently, both employer and employee pay a tax of 1.45%. (If you're self-employed, you must pay a tax of 2.9%.) High earners (individuals earning at least $200,000 and married couples earning $250,000 or more) pay an extra 0.9% known as the additional Medicare tax. These taxes primarily pay for Part A of Medicare. The other parts are paid for through premiums paid by those enrolled in Medicare, as well as by the government's general fund. As with most other things connected to retirement, the system is expected to experience strain as baby boomers retire. As with Social Security retirement benefits, though, there are several possible ways to deal with this growth in spending. Among them:

- Increase Medicare taxes
- Institute means testing, as is done for Medicaid

- Link Medicare to life expectancy
- Move toward online doctor visits rather than actual visits

Eventually some combination of these approaches, as well as others, will probably fix the issue of increased Medicare costs.

More Information

To find out more about what is covered by Medicare, call 1-800-633-4227 and ask for the publication called *Medicare & You: The Official US Government Medicare Handbook*. You can also order a copy at www.medicare.gov.

MEDICARE

Your Health in Retirement

As mentioned in the last entry, Medicare is divided into four parts. Each has its own focuses that add up to the whole of Medicare, and in the following section, you will learn more about what makes up each part. To begin with, let's start by looking at what Medicare covers in Part A.

PART A OF MEDICARE

Part A of Medicare, which focuses on hospital stays, covers the following:

- A semiprivate room
- Meals
- Nursing
- Hospital services

For a stay in the hospital of one to sixty days, you pay up to $1,632 (the 2024 deductible). For the next thirty days, you pay $408 per day. After day ninety, you pay $816 per day while using your sixty lifetime reserve days (sixty extra days that you can use any time you need to, but that never get replenished). Once you use up all your lifetime reserve days, you are responsible for all costs of the stay.

If, after three days in the hospital, you are moved to a skilled nursing facility, Medicare pays for the following:

- A semiprivate room
- Meals
- Nursing
- Rehabilitation
- Miscellaneous services

For the first twenty days in such a facility, you pay nothing. For days twenty-one through one hundred, you pay a $200 copay each day. After that, you pay all costs associated with remaining in the facility.

Medicare will also pay for some home-based healthcare services. These include:

- Part-time skilled nursing care
- Part-time home health aid services
- Physical and occupational therapy
- Speech therapy
- Certain medical equipment, such as wheelchairs, crutches, walkers, etc.

You pay 20% of the cost of medical equipment. All providers of this equipment and other services have to be certified by Medicare.

It's possible that if you have a terminal illness, you'll be placed in hospice care. Medicare Part A will cover the following elements of that care:

- Doctors' services
- Nursing
- Medical equipment
- Medical supplies

- Drugs to control your symptoms (you pay up to $5 for each prescription drug)
- Short-term hospital stay
- Therapy, both physical and speech
- Social worker services
- Dietary counseling
- Grief counseling for you and your family

Also, you may be responsible for paying 5% of the Medicare-approved amount for inpatient respite care.

Blood Is Covered

When you're in the hospital or a skilled nursing facility, it may be necessary for you to undergo a blood transfusion. If that's the case, Medicare Part A will pay for the blood after the first three pints. However, if you or someone you know donates three pints of blood, Medicare will pay for all the blood. If the provider gets the blood at no cost, you won't pay anything for it.

PART B OF MEDICARE

If you enroll in Part B of Medicare, you'll pay a monthly premium, just as you would for any insurance. As of 2024, the standard premium is $174.70 per month. If you get Social Security benefits, Railroad Retirement benefits, or Office of Personnel Management benefits, the premium will be deducted from the benefits. Otherwise, Medicare will send you a monthly bill.

If your income is above a certain amount, the size of your premium increases. The following table, adapted slightly from www.medicare.gov, shows how this increase works.

ANNUAL INCOME		AMOUNT YOU PAY
File Individual Tax Return	File Joint Tax Return	Monthly Premium
$103,000 or less	$206,000 or less	$174.70
Above $103,000 up to $129,000	Above $206,000 up to $258,000	$244.60
Above $129,000 up to $161,000	Above $258,000 up to $322,000	$349.40
Above $161,000 up to $193,000	Above $322,000 up to $386,000	$454.20
Above $193,000 up to $500,000	Above $386,000 up to $750,000	$559.00
$500,000 or more	$750,000 or more	$594.00

What Does It Cover?

Part B of Medicare is designed to cover doctor visits and everyday medical care. To this end, it will pay for:

- Visits to doctors who accept Medicare patients; this includes visits to hospitals, clinics, doctors' offices, or care in your home
- Medical equipment, on the same order as what's covered in Part A
- Tests done outside hospitals
- Preventive measures (for example, flu shots or vaccines)
- Visits to the emergency room

- Outpatient care and some inpatient care (for instance, if you're being kept under observation at a hospital)
- Ambulance and air rescue services
- Health counseling for lifestyle changes (giving up smoking or drinking, for example, or losing weight)

Medicare Abroad

Save for very rare circumstances, Medicare does not cover medical services performed outside of the United States. This is an important consideration for anyone contemplating retiring abroad. On the other hand, many destination countries for retirees have free or very inexpensive healthcare, so the loss of Medicare benefits doesn't matter much. If you're thinking of retiring abroad, be sure to check the status of healthcare in the country to which you're planning to retire.

PART C OF MEDICARE

This is often referred to as Medicare Advantage. It's where the government system of Medicare touches the private insurance business.

If you enroll in Medicare Part C, you sign up for a plan run by a private company. Pretty much, these plans will cover the same things as Medicare Parts A and B, but you may find that there are some advantages to the private plans. For example, they may charge you lower copays. The important thing is to pick the plan that works best for you.

Keep in mind that where you live will have something to do with the Medicare Advantage plan you choose (assuming you decide to go that route). In some rural areas, there aren't many plans available. People living in urban areas are likely to have many choices when it comes to medical insurance.

It's Not Written in Stone

If, having signed up for Part A and B, you change your mind and decide you'd rather go with one of the private plans in Part C (or vice versa) that's fine. You can switch during an enrollment period. Either way, you can change your mind.

The bulk of plans in Medicare Advantage are health maintenance organizations (HMOs) or preferred provider organizations (PPOs). Just like other kinds of healthcare insurance, they'll come with a list of doctors participating in their plan; if you see someone outside the network, you'll pay extra. One good thing about Medicare Advantage is that it caps the annual amount you'll spend out of pocket, something Medicare Parts A and B don't do. So, if you're concerned about your annual healthcare costs as well as your copay (in other words, you anticipate frequent visits to the doctor during the year), Part C may be the way to go. However, one thing to keep in mind is that like any private plan, those healthcare providers that are participants in Part C can go away—that is, they can decide to withdraw from participation in Part C. If that happens, you'll have to go back to Part A and B Medicare, at least until you can find another provider or insurer.

Enrolling in Medicare

You can sign up for Medicare starting three months before the date you turn sixty-five and ending three months after that date. Thereafter, you can sign up between January 1 and March 31 of each year. *But*—very important!—if you don't sign up for Part B when you first become eligible for it, your premiums will go up 10% for every twelve months you don't sign up thereafter. And that hike in your premiums will last you the rest of your life! So, if you do nothing else in that initial seven months around your sixty-fifth birthday, sign up for Part B.

PART D OF MEDICARE

As mentioned previously, Part D of Medicare is concerned with drug prescriptions. This is certainly an increasingly large part of any retiree's life. As with Part B, you pay a monthly premium. Part D plans vary from state to state, as do the premiums, but they generally range from $0 to $195 per month, with an average cost of $59 monthly. There is also a lot of variation in which drugs are covered by each plan, so make sure to check that your medications are covered before you commit.

Under Part D, you're required to pay whatever deductible your plan has (though some plans have no deductible). Additionally, you are responsible for copays until their total reaches a specific number ($5,030 in 2024). When you hit that number, you fall into what's called the "donut hole." In the donut hole, you'll pay no more than 25% of the cost of prescription drugs. When all your out-of-pocket costs for the year hit $8,000, you get out of the hole and go into catastrophic protection, during which 95% of your expenditures are paid by Medicare. When you reach the end of the year, the system resets and you start over again.

Sign Up for Part D

Just as with Part B, you're eligible to sign up for Part D for three months before the month of your sixty-fifth birthday, the month of your sixty-fifth birthday, and the three months after it. If you don't sign up in that initial period, your premium will go up—and stay that way. So as with Part B, sign up for Part D as soon as you become eligible.

The open enrollment period for Plan D lasts from October 15 to December 7 every year.

WHAT MEDICARE DOESN'T COVER

Although Medicare will pay an awful lot of your expenses in retirement, it doesn't cover some things. Expenses that you'll wind up paying for out of your own pocket include:

- **Glasses and eye care.** Medicare won't cover the cost of new frames and lenses or eye examinations. Nor does it cover the cost of contact lenses.
- **Dental care.** Although Medicare will cover some dental operations (usually ones that are performed while you're in the hospital), it won't cover routine visits to the dentist. Nor does it cover dentures.
- **Hearing aids.** Medicare won't cover routine hearing exams or the charge of getting and maintaining hearing aids.
- **Cosmetic surgery.** Medicare won't cover cosmetic surgery, including breast enlargement or reduction, unless it's the result of an illness or accident.

Chiropractors

Chiropractic care is covered under Part B—sort of. The manipulation of your spine, provided the service is given by a licensed chiropractor, is covered. You pay 20% of the cost plus your deductible. Medicare does *not* pay for tests ordered by the chiropractor, including X-rays, and therapy.

EXTRA HELP WITH PRESCRIPTION COSTS

If Drugs Are Too Expensive

Even with Medicare helping out, some medical costs are still soaring. One of the most pervasive of these is what people in the United States pay for prescription drugs. In the United States, the average person spends about $1,432 a year for prescribed medications.

Part of this is because the US uses more pharmaceuticals than the rest of the world. If you've got a condition, there's probably a pill you can take for it. Another reason is that in the United States drugs cost a lot more—sometimes as much as 30%–40% more than what they cost in places like France or Germany—because the pharmaceutical industry in America has gone unregulated in regard to price. But the Inflation Reduction Act of 2022 may bring about welcome changes for costs of drugs (specifically those with Medicare in certain parts).

Pharma CEOs Face Tough Questions and Fail

Three Big Pharma CEOs squirmed in front of the Senate Committee on Health, Education, Labor, and Pensions in February 2024. Senators asked the executives point-blank why their drug prices were significantly higher in the US than anywhere else in the world. They listed examples: the price for Keytruda, a cancer drug, is $100,000 higher in the US than in France, and the price for Eliquis (a blood thinner) is ten times more in the US than in Germany. The CEOs delivered many excuses, from claiming they weren't experts on drug pricing to blaming pharmaceutical benefit managers (middlemen). Bottom line: Americans shouldn't have to turn to crowdfunding campaigns to afford life-changing drugs.

HOW CAN YOU GET EXTRA HELP?

Recognizing these problems, Medicare offers the Low-Income Subsidy program, also called the Extra Help program, to help people
manage the cost of prescription drugs. However, this assistance is
only given to people with low incomes who might not be expected to
afford the medicine that many of them need.

This financial assistance, worth approximately $8,000 per year,
includes things such as prescription copays, monthly premiums, and
deductibles. To qualify for this assistance:

- You must be a resident of the United States.
- Your resources must be lower than $17,220 for an individual and
  $34,360 for a couple. By "resources" the SSA means any stocks
  or bonds you hold, and any money in your bank account(s). However, they don't include your house, car, or life insurance policy.
- Your annual income must be equal to or less than $22,590 for an
  individual and $30,660 for a couple.

As with most other Social Security–based programs, you can
apply for this assistance online by downloading and filling out SSA's
Application for Help with Medicare Prescription Drug Plan Cost
(SSA-1020). You can also call the agency at 1-800-772-1213.

A Little Bit of Extra Help

Even if your income or resources exceeds the limits outlined by
the prescription drug assistance program, it's possible you could
qualify for some extra financial help with your prescriptions. If you
or your spouse give financial support to someone else (typically a
child or a parent), or if you live in Alaska or Hawaii, you may qualify

for the Extra Help program. It's something worth discussing with your local Social Security office.

Avoid the Penalty

As previously mentioned, failure to enroll on time in Medicare Part D, the prescription drug part of the program, results in a penalty. However, if you apply for and receive Extra Help, that penalty won't apply.

MEDICARE SAVINGS PROGRAMS

While applying for Extra Help, you might also want to consider applying for the Medicare Savings Programs. These are administered by the states and are a way for you to save for anticipated medical expenses. When you fill out and return the form for Extra Help, the state automatically sends you information about the Medicare Savings Programs, unless you ask it not to.

There are four kinds of Medicare Savings Programs:

1. Qualified Medicare Beneficiary Program
2. Specified Low-Income Medicare Beneficiary Program
3. Qualifying Individual Program
4. Qualified Disabled and Working Individual Program

If you qualify for any of these, you automatically qualify for Extra Help in paying for your prescription drugs.

Qualified Medicare Beneficiary (QMB) Program

To qualify for this savings program, your monthly income must be equal to or less than $1,275 if you're single or $1,724 if you're married (for 2024). Your resources must amount to no more than $9,430 if you're single or $14,130 for couples. The program helps pay for Part A and Part B premiums as well as deductibles and copayments.

Specified Low-Income Medicare Beneficiary (SLMB) Program

To qualify for SLMB, your monthly income cannot exceed $1,526 (if you're married, the limit is $2,064) and your resources must be at or below $9,430 ($14,130 for married couples). SLMB helps pay for Medicare Part B expenses but none of the other parts. If you qualify for SLMB, you automatically get help with Part D, prescription drugs.

Qualifying Individual (QI) Program

Unlike the two programs just noted, you must apply for QI benefits every year; each year, priority will be given to those applicants who received QI benefits the previous year. If you qualify for Medicaid, you're ineligible for QI benefits. In 2024, to qualify for QI benefits, you must be limited to a monthly income of $1,715, or, if you're a married couple, to $2,320. Plus, your resources cannot total more than $9,430 if you're single or $14,130 if you're a married couple. The program helps pay for Part B expenses only, but as with QMB and SLMB, if you qualify for QI, you automatically qualify for assistance for Part D.

Qualified Disabled and Working Individual (QDWI) Program

To qualify for this program, you must:

- Be a working disabled person younger than sixty-five
- Not be getting medical assistance from the state in which you live
- Have lost your premium-free Part A coverage because you went back to work

Additionally, you must have a monthly income at or below $5,105 as an individual or $6,899 if you're a married couple. Your resources must not exceed $4,000 for individuals and $6,000 for married couples.

The program helps recipients pay for Part A, and as with the other three programs, if you qualify for it, you automatically qualify for Part D assistance.

If you think you qualify for one or more of these programs, call your state Medicare program.

PUTTING A CAP ON DRUG PRICES

The Inflation Reduction Act of 2022 gave Medicare the power to negotiate to reduce prices on specific prescription drugs. The agency will start with ten high-cost drugs in 2026 and increase to twenty drugs by 2029. The first round of drugs will include Eliquis, Jardiance, Xarelto, Januvia, Farxiga, Entresto, Enbrel, Imbruvica, Stelara, and Fiasp/NovoLog.

Companies that won't come to the negotiating table will have their drugs hit with a special sales tax of 95% (on the drug in question). The law also caps out-of-pocket drug costs for Medicare participants to $2,000 per year. Plus, the price of insulin will be capped at $35 per month for people on Medicare. The Act will pour $288 billion into prescription drug reforms. Medicare currently pays more than $216 billion annually for prescription drugs, and just ten medications account for 22% of those total costs. A Kaiser Family Foundation poll from July 2023 found that one in four Americans struggled to afford their prescription medications. The Inflation Reduction Act aims to get these costs under better control, but its full effects will not be seen for years.

MEDICARE ADVANTAGE

Independent Insurance Plans

If you go to Medicare's website (www.medicare.gov), you'll find a button that reads "Find health & drug plans." Clicking on that will take you to Medicare's plan finder, which is the easiest and best way to compare private health insurance plans that are available to you through Medicare Advantage.

PRIVATE PLANS

Medicare Advantage was discussed a bit earlier in this book. As you may remember, this is the name given to Part C of Medicare, and it gives the option of signing on to a private medical plan rather than Original Medicare, embodied in Parts A and B.

The first challenge to those interested in enrolling in Medicare Advantage is to choose between the wide variety of plans offered (although in some areas of the country, there is much less variety, making your choice easier but restricting your options at the same time). When you click on the "Find health & drug plans" button, you will go to the Medicare Plan Finder, where you can discover the plans available to you.

Plan Ratings

The Medicare Plan Finder also gives the plans a rating. If a plan is accompanied by a red warning sign, this means it's had low-quality ratings for three years in a row. You probably want to avoid such plans.

Clicking Through the Plans

Once on the Medicare Plan Finder page, enter your zip code to begin the process. You'll begin a four-step process:

1. First, the site will ask you some questions about your current coverage. You'll be asked if you currently have Original (or Traditional) Medicare, if you are on a Medicare Health Plan, and so on. You are also asked about the sort of help you get from Medicare to pay for your prescription drugs.
2. Next, you'll be asked to enter the names and dosages of the drugs that are currently prescribed for you.
3. In the next step, you'll be asked to choose the pharmacy or pharmacies where you would like to pick up your prescriptions. It's a good idea to enter at least two, so you can compare prices.
4. Finally, you're given an opportunity to refine your search. For example, you can ask for a listing of plans with high ratings and specific benefits. You can also ask for plans offered by a particular company or companies.

Once you've gone through all these steps and clicked the "Continue to Plan Results" button, the site will show you what plans are available in your area that meet your criteria. The information includes:

- Monthly drug and health premiums
- Deductibles and drug copay/coinsurance costs
- Health benefits, including out-of-pocket spending limits
- An estimate of annual health and drug costs

COMPARING PLANS

How you compare one plan to another depends on your priorities. Ask yourself the following questions to get an idea of what you want from your plan.

- Are you concerned about a high deductible?
- What is the highest monthly premium you can afford?
- Are you mostly concerned with your annual drug costs?

Write out a list of priorities that you need from your plan. Then, put them in the order of importance they have to you. Side by side, set out the benefits offered by each plan you're considering, again keeping them in their order of importance to you.

Once you've done this, you are a long way toward making your decision. However, before you do so, find out which plan provides the best Part D prescription drug coverage for the medications you currently take.

Cheap Isn't Always Better

Although you're on a fixed income now, resist the temptation to go for the cheapest healthcare plan. Too often, you get what you pay for, and your health isn't something to take chances with in retirement. Additionally, don't assume that if a plan is more expensive (for example, it has a higher premium) that it's necessarily better. Focus on the specific benefits and the numbers that are important to you.

Which Doctors?

At some point in your search for the right plan, spend a little time investigating which doctors accept which plans. It won't do you any good if you find a plan that's perfect for you but the only doctor who accepts it is a two-hour drive away. As mentioned earlier, this will be less of a problem for you if you live in an urban area, where there are more doctors to choose from. But if you live in an underpopulated part of the country, look at this question early in your search.

If you decide to enroll in a preferred provider organization (PPO) that allows you to go to any doctor, be aware that you'll have a higher copay for any doctor outside the plan's network. If you already have a doctor, you can call her or him and find out whether she or he accepts the plan you're interested in.

NOW YOU'RE READY TO ENROLL

Once you've picked your plan, there are three different ways to enroll:

1. On the Medicare website, click the "Enroll" button next to the plan you've chosen.
2. Call 1-800-633-4227, and someone from Medicare's helpline will walk you through the procedure.
3. Go to the plan's website and sign up there.

If you change your mind and decide you'd prefer to leave your plan and go back to Original Medicare (i.e., Parts A and B), you can disenroll. But you must do this during the open enrollment period, which is between January 1 and March 31 every year. However, if you signed up for Medicare at age sixty-five and this is your first year in the system, you can disenroll at any point within the first three months you signed up. You can also buy a Medigap policy within six months of switching back to Original Medicare.

It's possible you'll move during retirement and find yourself outside the area covered by your Medicare Advantage plan. No problem. You can re-enroll in a different plan or, if you can't find one you like, you can enroll in Original Medicare. You can also change your plan to another plan or to Original Medicare if you:

- Receive Extra Help with prescription drug costs
- Move in to or leave a skilled nursing facility
- Are a long-term resident in a nursing home

MEDIGAP

Whether you're enrolled in Medicare Advantage or in Original Medicare, it's entirely possible that there will be gaps in your coverage. In some cases, these may be things you can live with. In others, because of your past medical history or simply for peace of mind, they are not.

You can cover those gaps in Original Medicare by purchasing supplemental insurance, which is called Medigap. However, you'll have to pay all the costs of a Medigap plan.

Enrolling in a Medigap Plan

The first prerequisite for joining a Medigap plan is that you must be enrolled in Medicare—either in Part A or B. Medicare breaks down Medigap plans into ten different categories, labeled intermittently A through N. The following chart, found on the Medicare website, shows what these plans cover.

MEDIGAP BENEFITS	MEDIGAP PLANS									
	A	B	C	D	F	G	K	L	M	N
Part A coinsurance and hospital costs up to an additional 365 days after Medicare benefits are used up	Yes	Yes	Yes	Yes	Yes	Yes	Yes	Yes	Yes	Yes
Part B coinsurance or copayment	Yes	Yes	Yes	Yes	Yes	Yes	50%	75%	Yes	Yes
Blood (first 3 pints)	Yes	Yes	Yes	Yes	Yes	Yes	50%	75%	Yes	Yes
Part A hospice care coinsurance or copayment	Yes	Yes	Yes	Yes	Yes	Yes	50%	75%	Yes	Yes
Skilled nursing facility care coinsurance	No	No	Yes	Yes	Yes	Yes	50%	75%	Yes	Yes
Part A deductible	No	Yes	Yes	Yes	Yes	Yes	50%	75%	50%	Yes
Part B deductible	No	No	Yes	No	Yes	No	No	No	No	No
Part B excess charge	No	No	No	No	Yes	Yes	No	No	No	No
Foreign travel exchange (up to plan limits)	No	No	80%	80%	80%	80%	No	No	80%	80%
Out-of-pocket limit	N/A	N/A	N/A	N/A	N/A	N/A	$7,060	$3,530	N/A	N/A

You can buy a Medigap policy in the six-month period immediately after you turn sixty-five and are enrolled in Medicare Part B. If you need to buy such a policy, it's important that you do it then, because after the six months are up, you may not be able to purchase Medigap, and if you are, it will probably cost more.

MEDICAID

Helping Those in Poverty

While Medicare is a program designed to help everyone in retirement with medical costs, Medicaid is aimed specifically at families with low incomes. It works in conjunction with the Children's Health Insurance Program (CHIP), which provides health insurance for children whose parents have low incomes but make too much money to qualify for Medicaid.

As of November 2023, 85.8 million people were enrolled in Medicaid and CHIP. Of these, approximately 39 million are children. There was a substantial increase in enrollment in these programs following the passage of the Affordable Care Act in 2010.

WHERE DID IT COME FROM?

As has been previously mentioned, Medicaid, which debuted in 1965, was part of the Great Society social reforms instituted by the administration of President Lyndon Johnson.

The Great Society

In addition to strengthening Medicare and establishing Medicaid, the Great Society also included several important legislative initiatives. These included a series of civil rights acts that were designed to end systemic discrimination against African Americans; public education acts for providing financial aid to school districts across the country; and anti-poverty acts.

The Medicaid program has been expanded several times over the years. For instance, in 1970 it began to cover people who were in intermediate care facilities. Since Medicaid is operated at the discretion of the state governments, it took some time for all the states to implement this benefit. In 1986, Medicaid assistance was extended to undocumented workers under certain circumstances.

In 1991 the Medicaid Drug Rebate Program began to help manage the cost of prescription drugs, and in 2000 the Breast and Cervical Cancer Prevention and Treatment Act began covering any woman diagnosed with breast or cervical cancer.

After the Affordable Care Act passed in 2010, Medicaid began to offer a range of subsidies to help low-income people purchase health insurance. However, not all states are expanding subsidies in this way. (As of 2024, forty states plus Washington, DC, have expanded Medicare. Ten have decided not to do so.) To find out if your state is among those doing so, go to www.healthcare.gov/medicaid-chip/medicaid-expansion-and-you.

During the pandemic, Congress passed the American Rescue Plan Act (ARPA), which included incentives for states to expand Medicaid. The law added coverage for COVID-19 vaccines and treatment, increased federal matching funds for Medicaid, and provided funding for relief funds for rural Medicaid and CHIP providers.

The Consolidated Appropriations Act, which passed in December 2022, had provisions that affected Medicaid enrollment and funding. Beginning March 2023, continuous enrollment ended. The Act also phased down expanded federal funding that was put in place during the COVID-19 crisis, reducing those state subsidies through December 2023 and allowing states to disenroll participants.

WHO QUALIFIES FOR
MEDICAID BENEFITS?

Medicaid is a means-tested program, and eligibility is linked to poverty levels as determined by the federal government. However, there are other categories of people who may be eligible for Medicaid benefits. These beneficiaries include children from low-income families and low-income seniors. If you're enrolled for Supplemental Security Income (SSI), you're automatically enrolled in Medicaid.

Health Insurance Premium Payment (HIPP) Program

Some states operate a program called the Health Insurance Premium Payment Program (HIPP). This program allows people to enroll in a private insurance program, which will be paid for by Medicaid. Rules and regulations vary from state to state.

Because Medicaid is administered at the state level, qualifications for it vary. But in general, you will be required to show your income in relation to the federal poverty level (FPL). The FPL changes from year to year to take inflation into account. Some states also consider the assets you own, even if you're not using them now. Assets can include such things as investments, goods (such as gold or jewelry), and money in savings accounts. Most states list several ways in which you can qualify for Medicaid.

In addition to the issue of your income, to be eligible for Medicaid in a particular state you must:

- Live in the state
- Be a US citizen

Applying for Medicaid

Because of the state-by-state nature of Medicaid, you'll need to examine the specific requirements of the state in which you reside. You can find a list of contact addresses online at the Medicaid website: www.medicaid.gov/about-us/contact-us/contact-state-page.html. When applying, you'll need proof of citizenship. Appropriate documentation includes a US passport, birth certificate, or other materials that identify you as a US citizen. Visit the Medicaid website for details.

WHAT MEDICAID COVERS

Since Medicaid (unlike Medicare) assumes you have a very limited income, it covers a larger portion of medical expenses than does Medicare. Coverage varies by state and includes "musts" mandated by the federal government and optional benefits chosen by the state. Medicaid mandatory benefits include:

- Transportation to medical care
- Home health services
- Family planning services
- Out-of-pocket medical expenses (for example, doctor visits, physical therapy)
- More coverage than Medicare in long-term skilled nursing facilities

Depending on the state's plan, Medicaid may also cover things like eyeglasses, private duty nursing services, occupational therapy, dentures, and case management.

Children in Medicaid are eligible for comprehensive dental services, including maintenance and preventive measures. However, since many dentists don't participate in Medicaid, the number of people who actually use this service is limited.

State Health Insurance Assistance Program (SHIP)

Need advice about Medicaid, Medicare, or any other aspect of government-run healthcare programs? Contact your State Health Insurance Assistance Program (SHIP). Counseling is free, and it's enormously helpful in navigating the rocks and rapids of healthcare. You can find out more about the program online at www.shiptacenter.org.

SPEND-DOWN PROGRAMS

It's possible that you make too much money to qualify for Medicaid. Nonetheless, you may still be able to receive Medicaid benefits. If you spend your excess income (that is, income above and beyond what the limit is for Medicaid in your state) on medical bills, that's called a spend-down, and it could mean you're qualified for Medicaid.

Four groups of people qualify for Medicaid spend-downs:

1. Children under twenty-one years of age
2. Blind or disabled people
3. Adults over sixty-five years of age
4. Families in which at least one of the parents is dead, disabled, or out of work

Just to be clear, qualifying for spend-down doesn't mean that Medicaid will pay *all* your medical expenses. You're responsible for paying medical bills from your excess amount. After that, Medicaid will pick up your medical expenses. It's sort of like an insurance deductible.

What Bills Count?

The following medical bills can count toward a spend-down:

- Your bills
- Your spouse's bills
- Your child's bills
- The bills for a child who isn't living with you but for whom you have financial responsibility
- Past unpaid medical bills (how much past will vary from state to state)

Plus, you can count medical bills even if Medicaid doesn't cover them. However, bills for nonmedical services don't count.

If you are denied Medicaid, the Department of Social Services will send you a written notice telling you why your application has been rejected. It will also give you some information about the possibility of qualifying for a spend-down.

SOCIAL SECURITY AND YOUR RETIREMENT

Having a Rounded Financial Picture

As mentioned at the start of this book, a very large number of people rely entirely on Social Security to support them in retirement. This is a desolate picture, because unless you earned a great deal of money in your lifetime, your Social Security payments alone won't be large enough to provide you and your spouse with much of a retirement.

For 37% of men and 42% of women, Social Security represents more than half of their income (as of 2023). It made up at least 90% of income for 12% of men and 15% of women over sixty-five, and this number is not expected to decline. These figures, while not surprising given the economic struggles of many people, are also somewhat disturbing since Social Security wasn't designed to be anyone's only income in retirement. Rather, it was meant as a supplement to other income streams, helping older people to keep their heads above water and not sink into poverty. Social Security is an extremely important component of your retirement plan, but it's just that—one component.

However, there are some ways in which you can improve your financial situation, both before and after retirement. In doing your retirement planning, you can start by figuring out how to maximize your Social Security benefits. This was already discussed in some detail. Here and in the next few sections, let's talk about some other sources of retirement income that can supplement your Social Security benefits.

SAVINGS

Many Americans have very little or no retirement savings, and that's leading to a lot of seniors living in poverty. Unfortunately, it's not always easy to save for retirement. Millions of people don't have access to workplace retirement plans, especially people working at companies with fifty or fewer employees. Wage growth has lagged behind inflation and costs of living for decades. All of this makes it much harder for people to save enough to have financially secure retirements.

That said, some savings begun at *any* age is good. For many, distributions from their savings accounts can be very important supplements to Social Security benefits. So, if you can save anything, you'll be doing your future self a big favor.

HAVE A PLAN

One of the principal reasons people struggle financially in retirement is that they don't start planning for it soon enough. When you're twenty-two and just beginning your working career, it may seem impossible to envision the day forty-five years or so later when you close the door to your workplace for the last time. But the sooner you can start saving for retirement, the more time your money will have to grow.

To this end, there are several habits you can get into that will benefit you in anticipation of retirement:

- **Make and keep a budget.** Listing your income and your expenses gives you a very clear idea of where your money is going, and whether you want to make any changes. A budget will also help you to see what you can put aside in a savings account.

- **Decide what kind of retirement you want.** Many people, when they retire, remain exactly where they are and just stop going to work every morning. Other people want to travel, move to another state (perhaps to be closer to your children or grandchildren), work part-time, or go back to school. Each of these variations has different costs and different benefits. Do some research and find out what kind of retirement plan is right for you.

- **Take advantage of any employer-sponsored savings plans.** This applies particularly to 401(k) plans, and it's especially important if your employer matches your contribution. Such a contribution is really free money, and you should put yourself in a position to take full advantage of it. Find out the maximum amount your employer matches and contribute at least that percentage to your 401(k)—preferably more.

- **Set up your own retirement savings plan.** Even a small amount put aside every week or every month will add up and begin to grow on its own. Talk to your financial advisor about setting up an individual retirement account (IRA). Discuss with them the advantages and disadvantages of a Roth IRA as opposed to a traditional IRA, which have very different tax implications. Any amount you can save will make your life easier later.

- **Set up your own workplace plan if you're self-employed.** These plans, which include SEP-IRAs and solo 401(k) plans, allow you to stash much more than a traditional IRA would. This would give you the opportunity to build significant retirement savings while getting a current tax break.

- **Lead a mindful financial life.** Some books about retirement and savings will suggest things like giving up your weekly latte, but that's not what will make the difference. What will make the biggest difference is spending mindfully, which involves knowing how much you have available to spend and making conscious choices about where your money is going. It's easy to spend money without realizing it, so making more thoughtful choices will help you make sure you're using money for what you really want. Part of that will include some form of savings and investment so that your money can go to work for you, and you can build more wealth and financial security.

Social Security in the United Kingdom

Social Security in the UK, also called National Insurance, was first introduced in 1911. The post-war Labour government substantially expanded it, and despite significant blows during the Margaret Thatcher years, the system has survived to the present day. As of 2012–2013, the government estimates that the fund paid out £91.012 billion (approximately $115 billion) and took in £84.263 (approximately $107 billion). Every child receives a National Insurance number prior to her or his sixteenth birthday. For purposes of contributions, employees are divided into several categories, and employers are responsible for determining which category applies to a particular employee.

KEEPING TRACK OF
SOCIAL SECURITY

Recall from earlier sections the *my* Social Security account (www.ssa.gov/myaccount). Once you open an account at this site, you can regularly view your statement and see how the size of your benefit grows as you work more and more years. Your statement will also indicate how many zeros you need to get rid of—remember, your top thirty-five years of income are used to average your PIA, zeros included, so it's important to get them out of the way by working a full thirty-five years.

Make It a Family Decision

Since the issue of when to take your Social Security benefits is one that will affect your family, it's important to discuss it with them. Consider the issue of whether and when your spouse should take spousal benefits.

Your Expected Lifespan

No one really enjoys talking about her or his death, but it's important that you be realistic about your expected lifespan. The question of how long you can reasonably be expected to live has a big impact on the question of when to begin taking benefits. Consider such factors as heredity, your health history, and your personal habits, such as diet and exercise.

DELAYING YOUR BENEFITS

For many people, it makes sense to delay taking Social Security benefits until you reach your FRA and, if possible, until you reach age seventy. That's because your benefits will increase by 8% each year you delay taking them.

The problem, of course, is that it's very difficult for many people to go past age sixty-two without at least considering the option of starting their benefits, especially in a precarious economy. In some cases, you may have been laid off from work and are struggling to find employment. In others, you simply may not be able to work as much or as hard anymore. Or you may not want to keep working and decide to focus more on enjoying your life while you still have the time and energy to do that. Still, there is a financial incentive to wait as long as you can for increased benefits.

Age Discrimination

The 1967 Age Discrimination in Employment Act makes it illegal to discriminate against someone because of their age. Unfortunately, this is a rule that's honored more in the breach than in the observance. Nonetheless, be aware that when you're interviewing for a job it's illegal for the interviewer to ask you your age. If the issue does come up, the best thing to do is stress your many years of experience and how valuable that experience can be to your potential employer.

Here are some things you should consider as you work to delay your benefits as long as possible.

- **Downsize.** As many people approach retirement, they find it's easier to manage a smaller living space. A smaller home not only represents less of a physical challenge to maintain; it may also mean a smaller mortgage or rental payment. Downsizing also gives you an opportunity to declutter and streamline. So, there is less stuff to clean and maintain.
- **Move to a state with a lower cost of living.** Some states have lower costs of living than others, and by moving to another state, you may be able to substantially reduce your expenses. Of course, you'll need to consider other factors before making such

an impactful choice, but cost of living can be a big part of that decision.

- **Move to another country.** Many countries have substantially lower costs of living than the United States, especially nations in Latin America. As noted earlier, you can continue receiving your Social Security benefits in many places abroad. And one tremendous asset in many—though not all—of these countries is that healthcare is socialized and therefore free or available at a greatly reduced cost. In some countries such as Panama, English is effectively the second language; in other countries, English is widely spoken (although if you're going to live in another country, it would be good to learn the local language).

- **Find other sources of income.** These can range from teaching classes at your local community college (many colleges look for adjunct instructors with significant life experience) to offering your services online to creating a portfolio of income-producing investments. Remember, the more sources of income you have, the less you'll need to rely solely on Social Security in retirement.

- **Create a retirement budget.** Get in the habit of budgeting at the beginning of your working life. A retirement budget will help you figure out what income you need in your golden years and where the money can come from. By the time you get close to your full retirement age, you'll know what your benefits from Social Security will be if you retire at your FRA, or what it will be if you wait to claim until you're older. Keep in mind that when you retire, certain expenses will go away but others may crop up. For instance, you won't have to spend money commuting to work, nor will you be taking money from your paycheck to pay for a retirement account. And you won't be paying payroll taxes to help fund Social Security. On the other hand, you may spend more on entertainment, travel, and hobbies. And don't forget to include medical expenses, which tend to increase as you get older.

Healthcare in Retirement

Healthcare expenses are likely to be your biggest budget item during your retirement. For this reason, it's a good idea to remain on your employer's health plan for as long as possible. If you're forced to go off the plan (for example, because your employer doesn't offer health benefits to retirees from the company), you have some options. Chief among these is COBRA, which stands for Consolidated Omnibus Budget Reconciliation Act. COBRA gives you the option of continuing the same benefits you had when you were working, paid at the same rates as your employer. The downside: Those rates are very high.

ENTERING RETIREMENT

As you enter your retirement, you should have (ideally) at least three sources of income:

1. Social Security
2. Savings, whether in the form of IRAs or a 401(k)
3. Current income stream

These three income sources will help you achieve the kind of retirement you want. Current income streams could include things like part- or full-time work, income from nonretirement investment accounts, passive income streams like affiliate marketing, or rental income.

You also want to make sure you fully understand how required minimum distributions (RMDs) work so you can make proper withdrawals and avoid big tax penalties. Under the SECURE 2.0 Act, RMDs must begin at age seventy-three (which will increase to seventy-five by 2033). Your RMD will be based on your age and the balance of your traditional retirement accounts, and you have to withdraw at least that much from those accounts annually. If you don't, the IRS charges a 25% penalty on the amount you should have taken out.

USING A FINANCIAL PLANNER

Bringing in the Experts

By this point, maybe you've realized that planning your retirement, especially the Social Security aspect of it, is hard work. You have to learn a great deal, and even if you are a quick study, sound advice for planning your retirement is not something you can just pull off the Internet and use uncritically. For these reasons, you may want to consult a financial planner.

ASK AN EXPERT

There are numerous advantages to talking to a retirement and/or financial planning expert:

- These people think about retirement planning for a living. They know the ins and outs of Social Security and how to plan for retirement, and they can be relied upon to give you their best advice.
- They're likely to know the latest changes in government rules and regulations about Social Security benefits, and how those changes might affect retirement planning.
- They can help you with a long-term plan for retirement, so you don't stumble from financial crisis to financial crisis. Of course, it's up to you to actually carry out the plan, but a financial planner can help you see the road ahead.

WHO SHOULD YOU TALK TO?

There are plenty of financial advisors with websites; a lot of the sites are attractive and enticing. But you need to do a few things before you start contacting these service providers.

Decide What You Want

You can't ask anyone to do a job for you until you know what that job is. So, sit down and decide what exactly you want your financial counselor to do for you. For example, do you want them to:

- Suggest investment opportunities?
- Advise you when to take Social Security benefits?
- Help set up a savings budget?
- Assist you with estate planning?

Overall, it will help to make a list of the questions and requests you have for a financial advisor. So, do yourself (and your future advisor) a favor by seriously thinking about the sorts of things you need from them.

Social Security Questions

If you just have some questions about Social Security—how the system works or a specific question about your benefits—you probably don't need to go to the expense of hiring a financial advisor. You can contact the Social Security Administration at www.ssa.gov or call free at 1-800-772-1213. A representative of the SSA can take your call between 8:00 a.m. and 7:00 p.m. Monday through Friday. The SSA advises that phone waiting times are generally shorter in the middle of the week.

Do Your Research

Hiring a financial advisor is a serious business; after all, you're entrusting them with your money, which means you're entrusting them with your prospects for a financially safe and happy retirement. This is your future on the line, so there's no need to rush into things. Take your time and do your due diligence. Visit their website. See if they have been reviewed by Yelp or any other online review sites. Look at their qualifications. How long have they been in business? Do they say how many clients they've worked with? Have they worked with any businesses? If yes, which ones, and are they well known or familiar to you?

Be sure to get comfortable before you proceed. If you start to feel nervous, back off.

Many people are intimidated by the alphabet soup of initials that follow advisors' names. It's confusing, but the best thing is to hire someone who is a certified financial planner (CFP). Many other titles require only minimal certification; too often they're there to impress unwary potential clients. Someone who is a CFP has taken a course, passed an exam, has had three years of experience as a financial planner, and has signed on to a code of ethics.

If you want to check up on your possible advisor's record, you can do so by contacting the Securities and Exchange Commission (SEC). Ask to see the advisor's Form ADV, which must be filed with the SEC. That will tell you whether the person has had any brushes with the law or regulatory bodies.

Ask about Licenses

Your financial advisor must hold a core Series 6 or 7 license but could also hold a Series 63, Series 64, or Series 65 license. Confirm that she or he holds one of these licenses before proceeding. If you have questions about the licenses your planner holds, you can contact the Financial Industry Regulatory Authority (FINRA) for help. Their website is www.finra.org.

Ask about Payment

Before you begin doing business with your advisor, find out how much the services are going to cost, and how they expect to be paid. Some financial advisors are paid on a commission basis—that is, their fee is contingent on you purchasing a particular financial product. Others are paid a fee and a retainer. Both have advantages and disadvantages. In the case of a fee-based planner, they may charge you a percentage of your account, an hourly rate, or a flat fee for a consultation. Whatever the case, you need to know what this is going to cost you and then decide if it's worth it.

Look for Someone Well Rounded

If the only thing your advisor knows about is estate planning, they are not going to be very helpful to you in negotiating the complicated maze of Social Security. You want someone who has a broad grasp of personal finance so that you too can make sense of it.

Registered Representatives

If you're interested in purchasing stocks or bonds, you will want to contact a registered representative (RR). These individuals are authorized to buy and sell securities, and they are licensed through FINRA. They can offer you other financial services as well.

ESTABLISH A PLAN

At some point during the interview you conduct with your financial planner, ask them to show you examples of work they've done for other clients, with their clients' names blacked out. If these examples look satisfactory to you, ask them to sketch out a general retirement plan for you. They should be able to create one that includes income other than just Social Security. This may mean continuing to work in retirement (without, however, reaching an income level that triggers taxation of your benefits). Ultimately, their role is to help you establish an overall plan for retirement of which Social Security is a key component.

PLANNING FOR TOMORROW

Young People, Retirement, and Social Security

Like the beginning of this book says, when you start your first full-time job, Social Security and retirement are likely the last things on your mind. After all, you've probably got around forty years before you even become eligible for Social Security, and a few years past that before reaching your full retirement age.

The truth is, you're never too young to start thinking about your financial future. In fact, these days, it's more important than ever to do that. Experience of the Great Recession of 2008–2009 shows how easily nest eggs can be wiped out, almost overnight. But with enough time, they have a chance to rebound and replenish. On the other hand, a sound, long-term investing strategy can grow that nest egg—especially if you start it when you're young. Compounding of earnings is so powerful that if you start investing in your twenties, you can amass a large sum with little effort by the time you are in your sixties or seventies. This removes the problem of figuring out how to live solely on Social Security for the remainder of your life, and it goes a long way toward ensuring a financially secure retirement. All that's required is a basic understanding of retirement plans and the commitment to start now.

THE YOUNGER, THE BETTER

If you're in your twenties or thirties, you may feel like you have all the time in the world to invest for retirement. The younger you are when you start, the less you'll need to invest, thanks to the power of compounding and the length of time until retirement. You'll never have more time than you do right now, no matter how old you are. So, use the time that's on your side to help your money grow under its own momentum.

In the same way, don't wait until you turn sixty-two to start learning about the Social Security system. The earlier you study it and the more you know about it, the more you'll be able to anticipate the size of your benefit so that you can work to maximize it. You'll also be better prepared for unexpected events such as disability, the loss of a spouse, a child with disabilities, and so forth. The Social Security system (which, hopefully, you appreciate by now), is incredibly complex and can take a long time to understand—not to mention that Congress may take it into its head to change elements of the system again before you reach your full retirement age.

Invest While You're Young

It's difficult to think ahead to your retirement when you're young. There are so many things you want to do and so little money at your disposal. Yet, investing a relatively small amount of money in your twenties can save you from having to invest much more when you're in your forties and fifties such that you can live comfortably in retirement.

To illustrate, if you start contributing $750 a year (less than $15 a week) at the age of twenty-one and you earn 8% a year, at the age of sixty-five you'll have amassed $303,674. If you invest the same amount starting at age thirty, you'll have $143,367; and if you wait until age forty, you'll have only $59,438. It's not just that you've contributed more by starting earlier, though that is true. But your total contributions starting at age twenty-one come to $33,000 ($750 × 44 years), at age thirty it would be $26,250, and at age forty it would be $18,750. You can see that the earnings are much greater the sooner you start.

As noted in this book, Social Security is not designed to be your sole source of retirement income. Fortunately, you have retirement savings options you can use to provide you with additional sources of income once you stop working. Employers sponsor some of them; others are the do-it-yourself variety. Employer-sponsored plans fall into one of three categories: defined contribution, profit-sharing plans, and defined benefit. Most employer plans fall into the defined contribution category, and that's most likely what you'll have access to if your employer sponsors a plan.

EMPLOYER-SPONSORED RETIREMENT PLANS

Working with Benefits

According to the Bureau of Labor Statistics (BLS), around 70% of Americans working for private employers have access to employer-sponsored retirement plans, and around 53% participate. Workplace plans make it easy to participate through direct payroll deductions, offering employees a simple way to build up their retirement savings over time. These plans typically come with higher contribution limits than individual retirements plans like IRAs. Plus, many employers and plans offer matching contributions, where they put in extra money when you participate (which equates to basically free money for you).

DEFINED CONTRIBUTION PLANS

Employee-sponsored defined contribution plans focus on how much is going into them, but don't guarantee a specific dollar amount at retirement (like a pension would). How much you eventually receive depends on how much you and your employer contributed and how well your investments performed over the years. Your contributions, as well as the contributions made by your employer (if any), are always kept in an individual account in your name that you have control over.

With defined contribution plans, you're in the driver's seat when it comes to deciding how your money will be invested (at least to an extent). You'll choose from a predetermined set of stock or bond mutual funds, though some plans may also give you access to things like guaranteed funds, annuities, cash equivalents (like money market accounts), and stock in the company you work for. Your plan will stipulate how frequently you can change your investment choices, and there may be fees for doing so. Many plans allow you to manage your account online and make investment changes as often as you like.

One of the attractive features of defined contribution plans is that they're portable. If you change jobs, you can take your money with you. Here's a recap of the most common defined contribution plans:

- 401(k) plans, offered by private companies
- 403(b) plans, offered by nonprofit, tax-exempt employers, such as schools and colleges, hospitals, museums, and foundations
- 457 plans, offered by federal, state, and local government agencies and nonprofit organizations

Other defined contribution plans include Employee Stock Ownership Plans (ESOPs), money purchase plans, profit-sharing plans, Simplified Employee Pension (SEP) plans, Savings Incentive Match Plans for Employees (SIMPLEs), and Thrift Savings Plans (TSPs). These traditional plans all have one important thing in common: You pay no taxes on your contributions or your earnings until you withdraw the money. (It works differently if your employer offers a Roth-type plan, such as a Roth 401(k).)

401(K) PLANS

In 1978, Congress created the 401(k) plan, an employer-sponsored retirement plan that gives a special tax break to employees saving for retirement. Here's how the tax break works: If, for example, you contribute $2,000 a year and you're in the 28% federal tax bracket, you'll save $560 that year because the $2,000 is deducted from your pay before your taxes are calculated. If you live in one of the states where 401(k) contributions are tax-deferred, and you're in a 6% state income tax bracket, you'll save another $120 in state taxes, for a total savings of $680.

The bottom line is that you add $2,000 to your investment account but only $1,320 comes out of your pocket ($2,000 – $680 = $1,320) at the time. You don't pay taxes on your earnings until you withdraw them, so your investments grow faster as your untaxed earnings benefit from compounding.

Employer Match

To sweeten the pot even more, many employers match a certain percentage of your contributions, meaning they add extra money to your account for you. The amounts vary but a typical match is between fifty cents and $1 for every dollar you contribute, up to 6% of your salary. If your employer does offer a matching contribution, that's free money for you. So, it makes sense to participate in the plan and contribute at least up to the maximum match if you can. Where else are you going to find a guaranteed 100% return on your money (assuming your employer matches dollar for dollar)?

Contribution Limits

The IRS sets limits, adjusted annually for inflation, on how much you can contribute to a 401(k) plan each year. As of 2024, the limit was $23,000. The total of all contributions, including yours and your employer's, cannot exceed 100% of your compensation for the year, or $69,000, whichever is less.

Don't Leave Money on the Table

If you earn $30,000 and your employer matches 100% of your 401(k) contributions up to 6% of your salary, you'd have to contribute $1,800 per year ($30,000 × 0.06 = $1,800) to take full advantage of the employer match. Any less than that and you'd be leaving money on the table.

401(k) Vesting

You always own 100% of your own contributions to the plan. The employer match is often subject to vesting, which means you earn the right to it gradually, over several years of employment with the company. There are two types of vesting schedules. About half of all 401(k) plans have cliff vesting, where you don't own any of the matching contributions until you've worked for the company for a certain amount of time. The Tax Relief Reconciliation Act of 2001 shortened the maximum vesting schedule for cliff vesting to no more than three years. The other type of vesting schedule is graded vesting, where you own an increasing percentage of the employer match over several years. Under the Pension Protection Act of 2006, vesting must take place in no more than six years. A typical vesting schedule is 20% after the second year, 40% after the third year, 60% after the fourth year, 80% after the fifth year, and

100% after the sixth year. Remember, this applies only to employer matching contributions. Your money is always yours. But vesting is something you'll want to take into consideration if you're thinking about changing jobs.

Switching Jobs

The portability of 401(k) plans is a great feature, but what do you do with your money when you change jobs? You have four choices:

1. If you have over $5,000 in your account, you have the option of leaving your funds in your employer's plan.
2. You may be able to roll your balance over into your new employer's plan.
3. You can set up an individual IRA at a bank, through a broker, or directly with a mutual fund.
4. You withdraw the balance as cash, but that will generally have substantial tax implications.

401(k) Loans

If your 401(k) plan allows loans, you can borrow up to 50% of your vested balance, not to exceed $50,000. Loans typically must be repaid over no more than five years unless the funds are used to buy a first home. Interest rates are typically low—between one and three points above the prime rate. Because you pay yourself back instead of paying a creditor, 401(k) loans are touted as a great deal. Even the interest you pay goes back into your 401(k).

401(k) Loan Statistics

According to a report on the business and finance website *CNNMoney*, at the end of 2023 the average 401(k) account balance, net of loans, was a record $118,600, a leap of 14% from 2022.

But it's not as simple as it sounds. The first reason you should avoid borrowing from your 401(k) if possible is the tax consequences. Your repayments are not tax-sheltered. They're made with after-tax money. If your monthly payment is $200 and you're in the 28% federal tax bracket and a 6% state tax bracket, you'd have to make $303 to net enough to make the payment. Worse, when you retire and take withdrawals, you pay taxes on that money again. The second reason you shouldn't borrow from your 401(k) is the opportunity costs. The money that you borrow could be earning interest or appreciating if you left it in your plan. Over time, the impact on your 401(k) could be substantial.

If you have a loan balance when you leave your job, you may be required to repay the full loan immediately. If you don't, you'll owe federal and state income taxes on the amount you borrowed, plus a 10% early withdrawal penalty. Think carefully before borrowing your retirement funds, and do so only if you need the money for something important, like a down payment on a house, and you have no other alternatives.

403(B) AND 457 PLANS

Defined contribution plans used by nonprofit organizations are called 403(b) plans. They work very much like 401(k) plans. Your contributions are tax-deductible, and your earnings are tax-deferred until you take the money out at retirement. Like 401(k) plans, the amounts that you and your employer can contribute are limited by law.

Government agencies can establish their own defined contribution plans called 457 plans. Like 401(k) and 403(b) plans, they allow you to make tax-deductible contributions and your earnings grow tax-deferred until retirement. However, these plans fall under different rules, so there are some differences including catch-up contributions and early withdrawal penalties.

DEFINED BENEFIT PLANS

Employer-sponsored defined benefit plans, also known as pensions, provide a guaranteed income for the rest of your life after you retire. These are increasingly rare in today's job market, but some companies and government jobs still offer them. The amount varies depending on your years of service with the company, your salary, and your age at retirement. Your employer uses an actuarial formula to arrive at the amount to put into the fund each year to ensure there's enough to meet the future retirement needs of its employees. All funds are mingled in one account managed by your employer.

Vanishing Pension Plans

Pension plans have largely been replaced by defined contribution plans, which put more of the responsibility for retirement savings on you and less on your employer. To give you an idea of the rate at which this is happening: In 1975, 27.2 million employees were covered by pension plans; by 2020, only around 12 million employees (mainly those in unions) had access to pensions.

IRAS, HSAS, AND SELF-EMPLOYMENT

Create Your Own Retirement Adventure

Even if you don't have access to an employer-based retirement plan, you can still save for your retirement using tax-advantaged accounts. Whether your employer just doesn't offer one or you work for yourself, you have options that will help you create a more secure financial future. The type of account that will work best for you depends on your overall current situation, and as that changes over time your choices can change too. The first step will be understanding which retirement accounts are available for you, and then you can move forward to start building your nest egg.

INDIVIDUAL RETIREMENT ACCOUNTS

This book has discussed individual retirement accounts (or IRAs) before, but now it's time to go into them in more depth so you can see how they form an important supplement to your Social Security benefits in retirement planning.

IRAs have evolved since they were established more than forty years ago, and they now include variations such as Roth IRAs. Traditional IRAs provide the same tax-deferred benefits as 401(k) and similar employer-sponsored plans and give you the full power to decide where and how your funds will be invested.

If you have employment income, you can contribute up to $7,000 a year to an IRA ($8,000 if you're aged fifty or more). This figure includes *all* the money you contribute annually to *all* your IRAs, whether they're traditional, Roth, and so on. You can set up an IRA through most banks and financial institutions, or through a mutual fund company or broker. You can start making withdrawals at age fifty-nine and a half, and you must start doing so by age seventy and a half. Like 401(k) plans, a 10% penalty is placed on any funds you take out early unless you retire, need the money to pay medical expenses, or are disabled.

Contributing to an IRA doesn't make sense unless you're maximizing your contributions to your 401(k) or 403(b) plan by contributing the IRS limit. Take full advantage of these employer-sponsored defined contribution plans first and if you have money left to invest for retirement, consider IRAs. If you don't have access to an employer-sponsored plan, then by all means, invest as much as possible in IRAs.

Online Calculators

Use the online calculators at Charles Schwab to help you determine which IRA you're eligible for and whether you should convert your IRA to a Roth IRA. You can view them at www.schwab.com/retirement-planning-tools/retirement-calculator.

Traditional IRAs
If you are filing taxes as an individual, you have access to an employer retirement plan, and your annual income is less than $61,000, you can deduct all your IRA contributions up to the

contribution limit. If your income is between $61,000 and $71,000, you can deduct some of your IRA contributions. If you make more than $71,000, you can't take this deduction. (If you file as a married couple, your range is $98,000 to $118,000.) You have until April 15 to make an IRA contribution for the previous year, but make sure to do it before filing your income taxes. The IRS will check to make sure your contribution was made within the deadline.

Roth IRAs

There are several important distinctions between traditional IRAs and Roth IRAs. Traditional IRA contributions are tax-deductible (you use pre-tax dollars). Roth IRA contributions are not (you use post-tax dollars). Traditional IRAs grow tax-deferred until you withdraw the funds at retirement, and then they're taxed at your regular income tax rate. Roth IRA earnings are never taxed as long as you follow the rules. Roth IRAs also have no RMD requirements, and you always have access to your contributions (but not account earnings) without any tax issues. Unlike traditional IRAs, Roth IRAs are subject to income limits. If you make more money than the annual limit (which changes every year), you can't contribute to a Roth.

Choosing the Best IRA for You

It can be difficult to determine whether you'd come out ahead in the long run with a traditional or a Roth IRA. It depends on a few factors, such as how long before you retire, when you plan to start taking money out, and your tax bracket now and at retirement. There are benefits to Roth IRAs besides tax-free earnings. For one thing, you can always withdraw your contributions before retirement without owing taxes or penalties. Account earnings, however, are locked in until you reach age fifty-nine and a half *and* have had the account for at least five years. Follow all the rules and your withdrawals will be 100% tax-free. That means you'll have access to retirement funds that won't ever take a tax hit and won't be included in your taxable income. If you don't need the current tax break, Roth IRAs almost always make a better long-term choice because of the tax-free earnings and expanded access to your money. Of course, every situation is different, so it makes sense to talk to your accountant or financial advisor when choosing which type of IRA to open.

If You Make Too Much Money

If your income exceeds the limits for a deductible traditional IRA contribution, you can still put money in, but it won't lower your tax bill. With nondeductible IRAs, you'll get tax-deferred growth, and you won't have to pay tax on the portion of your withdrawals that you've already paid tax on.

Health Savings Accounts (HSAs)

You may not think a health savings account (HSA) belongs in the section with retirement plans, but it does. HSAs work sort of like IRAs only better. You put in pre-tax dollars, meaning you get a tax deduction for your contribution now. The money in the account grows tax-deferred. And if you use the money for qualified medical expenses, your withdrawals are tax-free. This is not one of those use-it-or-lose-it accounts either; it doesn't disappear if you don't use it by the end of the year. Instead, these accounts accumulate money over time until you need the money to cover medical bills. If you use the money for something else, you'll have to pay tax plus a penalty on the withdrawal amount. Once you turn sixty-five, those penalties won't apply anymore but the tax still will. Luckily, the list of qualified medical expenses is very long and includes things like deductibles and copays. It even includes menstrual products, over-the-counter medications, and trips to the dentist.

Unfortunately, you can only contribute to an HSA if you have a high deductible health plan (HDHP) and no one else claims you as a dependent on their taxes. Check your health plan documents carefully to make sure the plan qualifies you for an HSA before you contribute.

SELF-EMPLOYED RETIREMENT PLAN OPTIONS

If you have any self-employment income, even if it's for a side gig, you may be able to take advantage of the higher contribution limits for workplace retirement plans. Opening one can supercharge your tax-advantaged savings, so you can build future financial security more easily. To learn more about these plans and which might work best for your situation, visit the IRS website at www.IRS.gov.

SEP IRAs

A Simplified Employee Pension (SEP) IRA is a great and easy option for self-employed people to save for retirement. This plan works best when you don't have employees, but you can open one even if you do. Basically, a SEP sets up a separate IRA for each participant: you as the business owner and any eligible employees. Only the company can make contributions, and those contributions vest immediately. The biggest advantage of these plans for self-employed people is the high contribution limit: up to $69,000 (for 2024) or 25% of your net self-employment earnings (not including the contribution), whichever is less. Like personal IRAs, you can make your SEP contribution any time before the tax filing date (for example, April 15, 2025, for the 2024 contribution).

SIMPLE IRAs

Businesses with no more than one hundred employees and no other retirement plan can create a Savings Incentive Match Plan for Employees of Small Employers (SIMPLE) IRA. Like an SEP, these plans are easy to set up and administer. If you have a small business with employees, a SIMPLE IRA can be a good choice. Eligible employees can make pre-tax contributions of up to $16,000 (for 2024) and account earnings are tax-deferred. As the employer, you must either match 100% of employee contributions up to 3% of their salary, or contribute 2% of compensation for every eligible employee, even those who don't contribute to the plan. For yourself, you'd be an employee and employer, making your own contributions with the business matching.

KEOGH PLANS

Keoghs are tax-deferred retirement plans for people who have self-employment income. The IRS no longer uses the term "Keogh plan," but two types of defined contribution plans are still referred to as Keoghs by many people: profit-sharing and money purchase plans. Money purchase Keoghs require the same contribution each year even if you don't make a profit. Contributions are limited to the lesser of $69,000 (for 2024) or 25% of your self-employment income. These are complex plans and will require the services of an accountant or other professionals to establish, so consult your financial advisor before diving in.

CHOOSING THE RIGHT INVESTMENTS

How to Grow Your Money Without Really Trying

Whether you have an employer-based, self-employed, or individual retirement plan, the investment choices are up to you. Take the time to consider your options, factor in your personal risk tolerance and how many years it will be until you're ready to retire, and the choice will become clearer. What's most important is to invest in something, because if you don't actively choose investments your money won't have the same opportunity to grow.

STOCKS, BONDS, AND MUTUAL FUNDS

With retirement investing, it's important to think long term. Because retirement earnings grow tax-deferred and you have many years before you'll make withdrawals, retirement plans are best suited for your most aggressive investing, which means stocks and higher-risk mutual funds. The more time you have on your side, the more risk your portfolio can handle. If it experiences a downturn, there's plenty of time to recover. Diversify your portfolio to balance risk and reward, and you should come out far ahead in the long term. This doesn't mean you shouldn't choose your investments carefully. As you get closer to retirement, you'll start to balance out those high-risk, high-growth investments with some more stable income-producing securities like bonds and bond funds.

ESOPS

Again, it cannot be stressed enough: Don't put all your eggs in one basket. Thousands of employees who did so lost their entire retirement funds when their employer's stock lost value due to corruption or shaky accounting practices that hid serious financial problems. If company stock is the only option available to you in your 401(k) plan, look at other investment vehicles for some of your retirement savings.

ANNUITIES

When you buy an annuity, you sign a contract with an insurance company that stipulates the amount of your investment, whether you choose a fixed or variable rate for interest, the method of payment, and any fees. Fixed-rate annuities guarantee a specific interest rate for the life of the annuity. Interest rates on variable-rate annuities fluctuate with the ups and downs of the financial markets. You can invest with one lump-sum payment or build it gradually over time.

Your earnings grow tax-deferred, but the money you put in is not tax-deductible, so this is an investment best suited for someone who has taken full advantage of all the tax-deductible plans available and still has money left over to invest. It's unlikely that the average person in her or his twenties or thirties would choose this investment vehicle, but you should be aware of it in case an insurance agent attempts to sell you one. Remember: If you feel like someone is trying to push you into an investment that you don't fully understand, walk away.

Think about Your Social Security Future

Even though the day when you file for your Social Security benefits may be far in the future, you should give some thought to it now. Open a *my* Social Security account (www.ssa.gov/myaccount) and regularly check your statement. Watch as your annual earnings gradually replace those zeros and the size of your benefit grows. Think about what you want to do in retirement and how your Social Security benefits can help you. Be familiar with spousal benefits and disability benefits as well as things such as children with disability benefits. Life throws a lot of curve balls, and the more prepared you are for them, the better your chances are of knocking them out of the park.

FINDING HAPPINESS IN RETIREMENT

Will Your Retirement Be an Ending or a Beginning?

Up to this point, this book has discussed the mechanics of Social Security. However, keep in mind that Social Security is, after all, a means to an end. That end, for most beneficiaries, is a financially secure retirement. At the same time, in an age where life expectancy is increasing, retirees are finding new challenges to their retirement years. In the next few sections, this book will look at some of those challenges and provide information on how to rise above difficulties with the aid of Social Security.

The dictionary defines "retire" with depressing phrases such as "withdraw from the world," "disappear from sight," "seek seclusion or shelter," or even "go to bed." That may have been your father's, or your grandfather's, way to retire, but will it be yours? Not necessarily. The current generation is actively pursuing hobbies and business ventures into retirement.

WHAT TO CALL IT

For the better part of the past century, American society, with government and employer support, has been organized to "take care" of its vulnerable citizens—the very young and the elderly—who cannot care for themselves. Throughout history, people have worked until they were no longer able. In traditional societies, family units are comprised of succeeding generations—babies, parents, grandparents, maybe even great-grandparents, cousins, uncles, and aunts—where the very youngest and the oldest are cared for by more able family members. You can think of this as a family-based system of Social Security. This is not the retirement system that modern Americans know today.

Social Security currently considers full retirement age to be sixty-seven. This is, in effect, the age that our government says you can stop work voluntarily. Minus a tragic illness or major disability, reaching full retirement age doesn't necessarily mean you can't work. In fact, many seniors hope to push that retirement age back another five or ten years.

High Mental Functioning

A ten-year MacArthur Foundation study of people age seventy to eighty showed that those with the highest mental functioning had three traits in common: They were more mentally active, more physically active, and had a sense of their contribution to the world around them. The key to having the highest mental functioning is having all three traits, not just one.

There is a growing trend toward redefining the stage of adulthood between middle age and really old age. There are many commonly used terms to define this period of life that no longer seem to fit well, like golden years, mature, old age, aged, the elderly, life of leisure, or retirement.

Evolving terms associated with retirement years include: third-agers, my time, social entrepreneurship, or second adolescence.

Nancy Schlossberg calls this period "my time" because it follows the conclusion of major earlier adult responsibilities, such as raising children or holding down a job for thirty years or more. At this stage in life, personal interests and goals can be pursued unimpeded. Marc Freedman, head of Encore.org (formerly Civic Ventures) based in San Francisco and author of *The Big Shift: Navigating the New Stage Beyond Midlife*, offers a fresh view of what it means to be an older adult in America. He suggests that when you are living in the third age, you'll pursue lifelong learning, contributing to society, focusing on physical and spiritual health, integrating into a like-minded community, and dedicating time to get resources for this stage of life.

The senior centers that are organized to fill the hours of the bored and lonely with bingo games and shuffleboard no longer fill the bill. Don't think you need to sit on the sidelines while this new social dynamic unfolds. You can be front and center. Your body and mind can be stronger at sixty than your parents' were at sixty.

Social Security in Spain

Spain has one of the world's older systems of social welfare, dating back to 1883. It is now enshrined in the Spanish constitution, drafted and passed in 1978 after the fall of Francisco Franco. The system provides benefits for: healthcare, medical care for illness or accidents, maternity, death and survival, retirement, and disability.

Employers' contributions are substantially larger than those of employees. For example, for unemployment benefits the employee contributes 1.55%, while the employer contributes 5.5%.

As you move away from the full-time paid workforce, you can have a role shaping the institutions and services designed to help you have a happy and fulfilling third age. Some terrific work has already begun, but it will be up to you and your peers to take it to the next level. Meanwhile, new terminology will continue to pop up in the culture that tries to capture what the new retirement means.

YOUR DREAM RETIREMENT

Options for Ending Work

Do you have your own dream retirement planned out yet? Have you thought about how long you will be in retirement? Do you think you'll be doing the same activities in your eighties that you did in your sixties? If you are a forty-year-old reading this, statistically you have only lived half of your life. Do you plan to be in the employ of only one company by the time you decide to finally call it quits, or do you imagine traversing through a variety of career moves on a zigzag approach to your third age?

You may think you are far too busy with your current obligations to spend any amount of mental energy to forecast goals for what you will be doing in your fifties, sixties, seventies, eighties, and beyond. But the truth is, no matter the plans you make or the paths you take, with the aid of some thoughtful preparation you can embrace the ambiguity of your own post-work life and make it a good thing, not a paralyzing event.

Some scenarios for moving through the latter stages of your career include:

- **Winding down, but not out.** Would your employer permit you to move from a full-time work schedule to a part-time one?
- **Making a trial run.** How about taking a solid month off from work to test-drive being home 24/7? If someone else is in the house, will you be able to accommodate each other?
- **Deciding to change directions.** Do you have an entrepreneurial itch that has never been scratched? Ready to leave the factory and open a card store?

- **Redirecting your commitments.** Maybe you need a much-deserved rest, but could you envision taking on new responsibilities? More than likely, the board of a charity you care about in your community will welcome you with open arms.
- **Exploring your talents.** Is there an interest or skill you have been postponing developing because you simply didn't have time? Ready to audition for the community improv troupe or learn another language?
- **Engaging in the new.** Maybe you want to travel, but you cannot imagine idling away your days at a beach resort. As it so happens, there are many programs that encourage you to learn and contribute while visiting someplace new. So many uncharted paths are awaiting you. The key to success will be how well you cope with the changes you experience.

Challenges to a Part-Time Schedule

Easing into retirement by cutting your full-time work schedule to part-time can be tricky. You may be able to afford a reduced paycheck, but your coworkers may be unable to honor your part-time status. As a result, you may end up becoming a part-time volunteer.

It is a worthwhile exercise to observe others who are ahead of you on the path to their third age. Watch them and ask them what is working and what they would change if they could.

IF A DOOR CLOSES

Look for the Open Window

Sometimes retirement planning gets short-circuited. The technology company you began working for when you were in your late thirties grew and grew. Twenty years later it was bought by a bigger firm. You had stock options that were the major bulk of your retirement game plan until a dizzying downturn in the economy essentially vaporized not only your stock but the company itself, leaving you with ashes in your retirement account. Now what? This was not the scenario you had envisioned as you put in those twelve-hour days and traveled for your employer over weekends, all with a goal of building something great and realizing a juicy payoff at some point.

FLEXIBILITY IS KEY

The answer for this, or any radical change in your career path, is to remain flexible. Sure, the prospect of seeing your life savings wiped out is a legitimate reason for angst, grief, and anger. But you cannot stay in the valley of self-pity for long, because you need to pick yourself up and get going again. If you are going to find a new stream of income, you can do one of two things: Find someone to hire you or hire yourself.

Your first instinct upon losing a job could be to hurry up and find another that will put you right back on the track you left with similar responsibilities, perks, and pay. As well, of course, you will want to avoid having any of those zero-earning years that are, during your retirement, going to affect the size of your Social Security benefits.

Dealing with a Career Setback

A career setback has to be viewed as just that—a setback. It does not mean you will never earn money again, or that you will never be able to retire. What you need to hold on to is your sense of self-worth and a realistic view of your skills, experience, and talents.

The problem is that finding another job immediately may not be possible. If you lost your job as a result of an industry meltdown, there may not be jobs for your exact experience right now. You might have to think long and hard about making a major career twist, one that will carry you into and through the third age you may be approaching chronologically. This could be an opportunity to launch yourself into entirely new and exciting opportunities. Perhaps you should:

- Slow down the pace.
- Convert a hobby or favorite pastime into a business.
- Drop everything and move somewhere you'd prefer living.
- Take a year off and sail around the world.

Depending on your age, and what other financial resources you have salted away at the time of a career interruption, your choices can be either wide-open or driven by a need to rebuild savings and earn a reliable income.

Starting a Small Business

Many people who have lost their jobs consider starting small businesses. However, before starting a small business, you should do some research, draw up a detailed business plan, and above all, make sure you've got sufficient savings to support you while the business ramps up. Melinda Emerson, author of *Become Your Own Boss in 12 Months*, suggests that you, as a prospective entrepreneur, should have "enough money to support yourself or your family for a year or two, along with a year's worth of working capital."

If you encounter a career blowup when you are at an age that makes you less attractive in the marketplace (it may be ageist, but the older you are the harder it is to get hired for top jobs), you can figure out ways to repackage what you have to offer. You might have received the boot from a retailer, but your experience may be of keen interest to a market-research firm. Instead of working a predictable Monday to Friday schedule with set hours, you can reshape your work time into billable hours as a consultant. Don't be surprised to find you prefer this autonomy. Besides current income, it can carry you for many years into what would have formerly been considered leisure retirement years. Suddenly, the panic associated with job loss late in the game is replaced with an understanding that, as the rules loosen for how and when people retire, the risks associated with not having every duck in order at some arbitrary age are reduced.

BEING A FORWARD-THINKING RETIREE

People across the spectrum are experiencing a new way of defining what the later years of life should be like. One high-profile example is John Glenn, whose early career shot him into space in manned space missions. After retiring from the military and flying into space, Glenn ran for public office and served in the US Senate for the state of Ohio. Of all his contributions to society, he may best be remembered for his decision to apply for permission to train for, and join, the crew of a space flight in his seventies. He said, "Just because you're up in years some doesn't mean you don't have hopes and dreams and aspirations just as much as younger people do."

Other examples of older people continuing to contribute to society despite being the age of most retirees are at least three past US presidents. Bill Clinton and George H.W. Bush teamed up at the request of President George W. Bush to lead a worldwide relief and rebuilding effort for the areas devastated by a tsunami in South Asia. Jimmy Carter, who left office in 1980, went on to create The Atlanta Project (TAP), bringing rich and poor together to serve the community as a whole. He probably single-handedly put Habitat for Humanity on the map by donning a work apron and grabbing a hammer and some nails. He and his wife, Rosalynn, established The Carter Center. He became a diplomat "without portfolio," stepping into some of the stickiest political wickets on the planet and was able to bring warring parties to peaceful compromise, earning himself the Nobel Peace Prize along the way.

Consider Retraining

If you experience a work setback, you should take a good look at your qualities as a member of the workforce. As you contemplate a new work direction, you may need to take a self-inventory of what kind of training or education would make you a more attractive employee—or give you the tools to start your own business. Even if you've reached retirement age and elect to begin taking your Social Security benefits, retraining can open possibilities for creating new streams of income in retirement—something that's very desirable.

If President Carter felt he had left office with a job unfinished, he found new spheres in which to express his many talents. In the process he has, with his wife, shared his experience of reinventing himself later in life by authoring two books: *Everything to Gain: Making the Most of the Rest of Your Life* and *The Virtues of Aging*. His view may best be summed up with his quote: "Retirement has not been the end but a new beginning."

THE NEW RETIREMENT

No Rocking Chairs for Baby Boomers and Gen Xers

When it comes to retirement these days, tear up the script and throw out the rule book. Old age never looked so good. One thing about baby boomers: They never saw a mold they didn't want to break. A lifetime of rewriting the script for how life should be lived is not going to end with a simple retirement. The values that are important to baby boomers will carry through every decade of their lives and will change the way the generations that follow think of retirement.

Gen Xers have a different perspective: They're worried retirement could be a struggle. This is the first generation to be relying mainly on their own savings through 401(k)s and other self-funded plans rather than pensions. They don't trust Social Security will be there for them—at least, not in the way it has consistently supported retirees in the past. And many of them are still burdened with overwhelming student loan debt, making it harder to save as much as they want to. But there's good news too. This is a financially savvy generation, with more than 80% of them having a good handle on subjects like investing, money management, and taxes. They're prepared to work a little longer and take more risk in their portfolios to ramp up the reward potential.

BOOMER AND GEN X PERSPECTIVES

The same spirit of rugged individualism that launched astronauts into outer space is fully ingrained in the American boomer psyche. That powerful combination of optimism and drive has been embraced by the boomer generation (born between 1946 and 1964) as they leave behind their careers. Boomers might want a respite from hard-charging careers, but it won't be long before they trade in their trader desks for tracking global warming trends in their new-found free time.

Gen Xers have a wildly different approach, seeking more security and predictability in their lives. Many plan to continue working at least part-time even after retirement, both for a sense of continuity and financial stability. They want this work to be important, fulfilling, and flexible so it adds to their lives and sense of purpose.

PLAN FOR INCOME, PLAN FOR LIVING

To successfully retire, it takes discipline and diligent management of savings and investments. You must stitch together the income sources needed to carry you for perhaps decades. One of the key lessons you hopefully learned is that Social Security is an important—perhaps *the* most important—element in your financial planning for retirement. You should remain doggedly committed to "paying yourself" every pay period and, most importantly, not give in to the temptation to spend money if it passes through your hands in transition from one retirement plan to another. Simply put, you need to turn time to your advantage. And you do this by putting money into retirement accounts right from the start of your working days and leaving them there to grow.

You should look to maximize your Social Security benefits by not beginning your benefits until you reach your full retirement age or, if possible, until age seventy. You should also be aware of other Social Security strategies and issues, such as the retroactive lump-sum provision and the Windfall Elimination Provision.

All these things contribute to your retirement success, which is the overall goal here.

BUDGET

The best way to plan for retirement is to draw up a budget. The kind of budget you create will depend very much on what kind of retirement you want to have. To do this, create an easy chart.

In one column put your projected monthly Social Security benefit (more on how to arrive at this number shortly). Then, add revenue from your other projected income streams. These can include annual distributions from your 401(k) and IRA, divided by twelve; money from any freelance work you plan to do in retirement; annuities; investment income—anything to put on the plus side of the ledger.

In the second column, make a comprehensive list of monthly expenses: rent or mortgage, gas, food, utilities, credit card bills, and so on.

In this way, you can get a clearer picture of whether your retirement is financially feasible as you envision it, and also what sort of role Social Security plays in it. Social Security is important, there's no question. But when it comes to a financially secure retirement, it shouldn't be your only reliable source of income.

Life Planning

As stated before, the old norms for defining retirement are eroding—the exciting evolution underway is bringing new life to what had been considered the quiet years of old age. You will be blessed with the time and hopefully the energy to pursue your interests during your post-work years. Consequently, you will need to do some long-term planning for how you will live in retirement. Just as with financial planning, life planning requires thoughtful deliberation of options. Before you can pick from the choices that appeal to you, you should do some research to learn more about your areas of interest. These can cover a range of possibilities and may include traveling (for any reason), developing nascent interests, volunteering, taking classes to learn new skills, working on political issues, being a mentor, or organizing social events for your community and beyond.

When you are deep in the trenches of your workday life, you may be so busy that you can only just find enough time for your job and personal life, never mind plan for the future. Yet before you know it, your friends are building a little vacation house with a goal of moving there full-time in retirement; you realize that your kids can drive themselves to their many activities; and you are nearing the number of years worked at your firm to become fully vested in the retirement plan. Suddenly it's time to take a look ahead. As you take in the potential of the decades ahead, start sketching out a vision of the following dimensions of your life:

- Housing options for each decade after fifty
- "Downtime" you'll need daily and weekly, and what form it might take
- Activities for relaxation, stimulation, or escape
- Components of a healthy lifestyle
- Social life
- Spiritual life
- Family obligations

It is no secret that the expectations for job performance have ramped up to red zone levels of intensity for many people. With instant access to information online, the ease of shooting texts or emails back and forth, and the demands of social media, cultural norms for communication have shifted to put intense emphasis on speed. Taking time to weigh options, reflecting upon a response before firing it off, or having the time to gather all relevant information to formulate the solution to your problem is becoming archaic.

If you are going to do a good job of getting your mind, as well as your wallet, prepared for retirement, you somehow will need to find a way to carve out time and space for reflecting upon, and planning for, how you expect your transition out of work to go. Jeri Sedlar and Rick Miners wrote a book together called *Don't Retire, Rewire!* In it they offer the following list of questions to ask yourself as a start for discovering what shape your retirement might take:

1. What picture comes to mind when you imagine being retired?
2. What do you anticipate adding to your life in retirement?
3. What do you picture giving up?
4. Do you have ideas for what your retirement should be?
5. How about not retiring? What image comes to mind? Something positive? Something negative?
6. Have you observed retirements of friends? Parents? Relatives?
7. What parts of what you have seen would you emulate, or do differently?

Counsel for Financial and Life Planning

This book previously touched upon what you should do to select a financial planning advisor to help you cope with Social Security and overall retirement planning. In much the same way, you can seek counsel for the life planning part of your coming decades.

As a reminder, your financial planning advisor may ask you to articulate the concrete needs of your retirement:

- Will you be able to live where you are now? For how long?
- How will your healthcare needs be met?
- Do you need tax planning for your estate?
- What will be your income sources?

Your advisor will then help you find the way to put the dollars together for those goals. This financial expert may not have the skills to tease out the more esoteric dimensions of thinking through what shape your retirement might take. For that, you will need to do some life planning. A life coach, goal-oriented journal, books, trends in media, or talking to retired people may help you develop a retirement life plan.

You can find many websites that address dimensions of retirement other than those that are exclusively financial. A few examples are:

- https://retiredamericans.org
- www.aarp.com
- www.forbes.com/forbes
- https://money.usnews.com/money/retirement

Creating a retirement life plan will be an ongoing process, continuing even once you are in retirement. The more effort you put into preparing yourself by declaring your dreams and expectations (even if only in the privacy of a journal), the more likely you will come up with a game plan you can follow.

When Two Are Involved

If you have a spouse or partner, you will need to create both individual life plans and a team plan. If you do not expect to be retiring around the same time, there may be some significant juggling of goals and expectations, or at least defining their timelines. Some instances in which couples may be out of sync with their retirement launches are:

- When there is an age spread of ten or more years
- When one partner has had a later start getting into a particular retirement plan (in a school system, for instance) and needs to put in the requisite years to reap the benefits
- When a stay-at-home spouse takes on employment around the same time the other spouse gets ready to sell a business and get out of the workaday world
- When one partner needs to stop working due to a serious health problem or disability

It is hard enough trying to get your own life sorted out, and it is all that much harder to manage the complexity of creating workable plans for two people. This is all the more reason you must treat the life-planning facet of your retirement with the same care and seriousness you apply to financial preparedness.

Go for the Discount

Don't be shy about grabbing every possible senior discount you can. From movie tickets to car washes, you can find ways to save. Some of the biggest retailers offer senior discounts on a midweek day. Plan your big purchases accordingly. Joining organizations such as the American Automobile Association (AAA) or American Association of Retired Persons (AARP) can give you preferred pricing in a host of places too.

RESPONDING TO SOCIETAL PROBLEMS

In this book you've learned about two government programs that were created to help individuals and families. They are, of course:

- Social Security, which supports older and disabled Americans who cannot work
- Medicare/Medicaid, which provide medical insurance for older or poor Americans

Other initiatives, either private or public, facilitate people giving their time to help those who need it, both in this country and internationally. Among some of the better known are:

- Peace Corps: www.peacecorps.gov
- AmeriCorps: https://americorps.gov/serve
- Habitat for Humanity: www.habitat.org

- Doctors Without Borders: www.doctorswithoutborders.org
- City Year: www.cityyear.org
- American Red Cross: www.redcross.org

Service organizations offer individuals like yourself structured opportunities to offer a helping hand to those in need. Through them, you can help alleviate suffering or provide basic human needs like food, shelter, or healthcare.

Giving Back to Get Back

Working closely with people suffering a true need such as hunger can educate the volunteer about the root causes of the problem. The person being helped has as much to give by sharing the experience of her need with the person offering assistance. She is an expert in the topic of her need.

You and your compatriots are more than likely going to be the architects of entirely new ways of responding to social problems, bringing fresh views and an abundance of "can-do" energy to the task of conquering stubborn issues like homelessness and chronic hunger. You are accustomed to breaking the rules, thinking outside the box, doing it your way. You're not going to stop seeking better ways now.

DOWN BUT NOT OUT

Life transitions don't always go smoothly, even with the best of planning. Sometimes events happen that will force you to adjust the grand plan. You may think you are perfectly positioned to leave your company at your full retirement age with a pretty good nest egg. You may have been disciplined, saving enough funds to enable you to live work-free and go on a safari, fund family reunions at a Disney theme park, or chuck it all and sail around the world. This plan might be ditched when, in your late fifties but well before retirement, you experience any of the following sudden events:

- Your company has massive layoffs, which includes you.
- You become disabled, limiting your mobility drastically.
- You have to assume guardianship for a family member.
- Your 401(k) investments are wiped out.

As devastating as any of these situations would be, you can work your way through them, or any other setback, developing a Plan B. Americans are blessed with a broad streak of optimism. If you suffer a major financial setback in the years encroaching upon retirement, you may panic, thinking that you do not have enough years left to recoup what you have lost. The financial loss may mean you have to abandon plans for your gilded retirement life. It might further mean you have to defer your departure from the ranks of the rank and file for a few more years. Depending on other resources available to you, including Social Security and other savings, you may be able to proceed with your retirement timeline, but find you will be swimming at the community pool and not at the beaches of Antigua. Look at the bright side—at least you will not be tied to a job.

Forced Into Taking Early Benefits

This book has advised against taking early Social Security benefits when you turn sixty-two. Still, that's when a majority of beneficiaries start taking them. Often the reason is a layoff. If this happens to you, taking early benefits may be your only option. But it's not one to rush into, since it will permanently fix your monthly benefit at a lower level. Carefully consider all other options before taking this step and see if it's at all possible to hold on financially until you reach your full retirement age.

BOUNCING BACK

Most setbacks are not insurmountable. They definitely change the picture, challenging you to come up with coping strategies. When you suffer a financial blow, your basic choices boil down to spending less, saving more, or both.

Spending less may seem unappealing at first because you feel you are being deprived of a life you thought you had all figured out. But by using a little creativity you should be able to construct a joyful, enriching, and full life. Just because you cannot have a Rolex doesn't mean you cannot have a watch.

INDEX